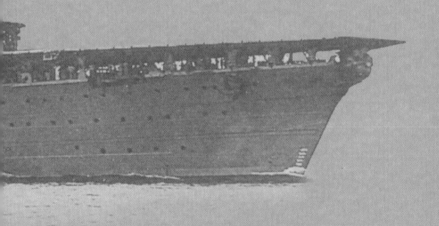

LEGENDS OF WARFARE
NAVAL

Kaga and Akagi
Aircract Carriers in the Imperial Japanese Navy

HANS LENGERER & LARS AHLBERG

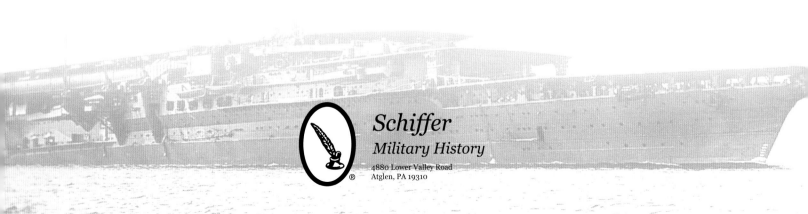

Schiffer
Military History

4880 Lower Valley Road
Atglen, PA 19310

Designed by Alexa Harris
Cover design by Jack Chappell
Type set in Impact/Universe Lt Sd/Minion Pro
ISBN: 978-0-7643-6893-6
Printed in India

Published by Schiffer Publishing, Ltd.
4880 Lower Valley Road
Atglen, PA 19310
Phone: (610) 593-1777; Fax: (610) 593-2002
Email: info@schifferbooks.com
Web: www.schifferbooks.com

For our complete selection of fine books on this and related subjects, please visit our website at www.schifferbooks.com. You may also write for a free catalog.

Schiffer Publishing's titles are available at special discounts for bulk purchases for sales promotions or premiums. Special editions, including personalized covers, corporate imprints, and excerpts, can be created in large quantities for special needs. For more information, contact the publisher.

We are always looking for people to write books on new and related subjects. If you have an idea for a book, please contact us at proposals@schifferbooks.com.

Acknowledgments

In compiling this brief history of the aircraft carriers *Akagi* and *Kaga*, we are indebted to the following individuals who over a long period of time have given invaluable help in our research of the Imperial Japanese Navy: Messrs. Endō Akira, Fujita Takashi, Hayashi Yoshikazu, Ishibashi Takao, Itani Jirō, Iwasaki Yutaka, Izumi Kōzō, Kamakura Takumi, Kimata Jirō, Kitagawa Ken'ichi, Kitamura Kunio, Koike Naohiko, Maejima Hajime, Mizutani Kiyotaka, Morino Tetsuo, Naitō Hatsuho (via Itani), Nakagawa Tsutomu, Takagi Hiroshi, Takahashi Shigeo, Takasu Kōichi, Tamura Toshio, Todaka Kazushige, Tsuda Fumio, and Tsukamoto Hideki.

Special thanks go to Messrs. Wilhelm Besch, Michael Wünschmann, Jürg Tischhauser, and Waldemar Trojca for drawings.

All photos are from the authors' collections unless otherwise noted.

Contents

CHAPTER 1   From the Washington Arms Limitation Treaty (1922)

              until the London Arms Limitation Treaty (1930)   004

CHAPTER 2   The Standard Aircraft Carriers Akagi and Kaga   007

CHAPTER 3   Outline Description of Akagi   022

CHAPTER 4   Outline Description of Kaga   039

CHAPTER 5   Defects Affecting Their Operational Value   053

CHAPTER 6   Modernization of Kaga   055

CHAPTER 7   Modernization of Akagi   064

CHAPTER 8   Evaluation of the Conversions and Identification Marks   077

CHAPTER 9   Shipbuilding Conception after the Decision to Convert

              Akagi and Kaga into Aircraft Carriers   080

CHAPTER 10   Operational Histories   083

              Endnotes   126

From the Washington Arms Limitation Treaty (1922) until the London Arms Limitation Treaty (1930)

The Washington Arms Limitation Treaty and Its Effect on the Construction of Aircraft Carriers

When the United States accelerated its shipbuilding with the execution of the shipbuilding law of August 29, 1916—the so-called Three-Year Planning—after the termination of World War I, the goal was to possess a navy "second to none." But the mood of disarmament after the "Great War," with its heavy loss of lives and great destruction, grew in company with the pressure of the naval expenditures on the national finances, but the successful conclusion of an arms limitation treaty by the League of Nations seemed not to be obtainable—the United States was not a member. In this situation the newly elected president, Warren G. Harding, backed by the opinion of the US Senate and the British government, unofficially proposed a conference to Japan, Britain, France, and Italy on July 10, 1921,[1] to deal with "arms limitation as well as the Pacific and South Asia problems."[2] After the unofficial proposal, the Armament Limitation Countermeasure Research Board (Gunji Seigen Taisaku Kenkyūkai) submitted one more report[3] to the Imperial Japanese Navy (IJN) minister, Katō Tomosaburō, in which, as advantages of a disarmament treaty, the following were stressed: (1) avoidance of a naval race,[4] (2) reduction of the burden on the nation, (3) limitation, to some degree, of the naval power of the hypothetical enemy, (4) maintenance of their own naval force at a certain level, (5) obtaining a kind of balance owing to the decided ratio, so that neither the IJN nor the hypothetical enemy would be menaced by a new shipbuilding program, and (6) facilitation of the operation planning due to the ratio.

Disadvantages were also mentioned—mainly as follows: (1) The limitation of the national defense power with the agreement of the hypothetical enemy hurts the principle of independent national power, and (2) in case of concluding an unfavorable treaty, the national defense of the empire may be endangered—but reason was victorious in the end, and the "Washington system" was established. The Washington Conference opened on November 12, 1921, and ended with the signature of the Washington Arms Limitation Treaty by the plenipotentiaries of the United States, Britain, Japan, France, and Italy on February 6, 1922. This "Five-Power Treaty" was ratified in Japan on August 5, 1922, was promulgated as "Treaty #2," and became effective on August 17, 1923. Supplemented by the London Arms Limitation Treaty of 1930, it regulated warship construction comparatively successfully until its termination on December 31, 1936.

The treaty was divided into three chapters: chapter I dealt with "General Rules about Naval Arms Limitations"; chapter II, "Regulations on the Execution of the Treaty—Appointed Times"; and chapter III contained "Various Regulations." These three chapters were divided into twenty-four articles and four paragraphs. The latter, in chapter II, were (1) names of the capital ships, which may be maintained by the signatory powers, (2) regulations on the scrapping of warships, (3) replacement (of capital ships and aircraft carriers), (4) definitions (capital ship, aircraft carrier, and standard displacement).

The following table shows the principal regulations for capital ships (battleships and battle cruisers) and aircraft carriers, the latter being the only warship type for which regulations were decided. All warships except the two aforementioned types were subsumed under "auxiliary vessels" and had only two limitations—tonnage and maximum gun caliber—according to articles 11 and 12.

Principal Regulations of the Washington Arms Limitation Treaty (1922)				
	Japan	**Britain**	**USA**	**France**	**Italy**
Capital ships				
Total tonnage	315,000 (3)	525,000 (5)	525,000 (5)	175,000 (1.75)	175,000 (1.75)
Single ship maximum tonnage	35,000 tons standard				
Maximum main gun caliber	16" (406 mm)				
Aircraft carriers				
Total tonnage	81,000 (3)	135,000 (5)	135,000 (5)	60.000 (1.75)	60,000 (1.75)
Single ship maximum tonnage	27,000 tons standard; each country permitted to build two aircraft carriers up to 33,000 tons provided the allotted total tonnage is not exceeded. Two abolished capital ships can be reconstructed for this purpose to save expenses				
Maximum main gun caliber	Should be below 8" (203.2 mm). The number of guns of more than 6" (152.4 mm) caliber should be within ten, and the carrier, which does not exceed 27,000 tons, should have fewer than eight guns of 6" caliber				
Other warship types				
Total tonnage	no limitation				
Single ship maximum tonnage	10,000 tons standard				
Maximum main gun caliber	8" (203.2 mm)				

Notes:
(1) Number in parenthesis means ratio between the countries.
(2) Building stop of capital ships for ten years. Capital ships could be modernized by reinforcing the protective deck and fitting of bulges against aerial and submarine attacks within the limit of 3,000 tons standard (3,048 metric tons).
(3) Aircraft carriers displacing less than 10,000 tons standard were not included in this category by the regulations.
(4) The standard displacement was defined in the treaty. Roughly: completed ships with full complement and every preparation for navigation but without fuel and reserve boiler water. Expressed in British tons of 2,240 pounds corresponding to 1,016 kg = 1,016 metric tons. Very important regulation for the design of warships and introduced to attain comparable data.

The initial proposal by Charles Evan Hughes on November 12, 1921, for the total tonnage of aircraft carriers had been 80,000 tons each for the United States and Britain, 48,000 tons for Japan, and 28,000 tons each for France and Italy. When the problem of the aircraft carrier was discussed on December 28, 1921, Italy (Vice Admiral Alfredo Acton wanted two standard aircraft carriers, which are 27,000-ton ships), Britain (Lord Arthur Lee required five standard aircraft carriers), France (Vice Admiral Ferdinand de Bon stressed the necessity of three standard aircraft carriers but was willing to accept 60,000 tons), and Japan rejected the American proposal. Admiral Katō subscribed to the Italian view (the 28,000-ton maximum for Italy would have permitted the building of one standard aircraft carrier, but if this ship was sunk, Italy would have no aircraft carrier for several years) and also to the British view (the proposals in view of the qualitative limitation of the single ship are necessary; the ratios of the capital ships[5] should be applied to the aircraft carriers too, because this type had developed to become an integral part of a modern fleet, and Britain required five standard aircraft carriers for defense) and

insisted on an 81,000-ton maximum for Japan because the defense of Japan required at least three standard aircraft carriers due to its insular position, and the maximum displacement per ship have to be taken advantage of. He also agreed to a proportional increase in the total displacement tonnage of the US and British aircraft carriers.

After pros and cons were presented, a new scheme was proposed, and the chief of the delegations eventually agreed to the total tonnages and ratios of article VII, as stated in the table.[6]

Chapter II, part 4, paragraph 2, defined the aircraft carrier as a warship of more than 10,000 tons of standard displacement, designed for the particular and exclusive purpose of carrying aircraft and constructed in such a way that aircraft were able to take off and land on it. In addition, it could be neither designed nor constructed to carry a gun armament stronger than permitted in articles IX or X, depending on the case (standard aircraft carrier or 33,000-ton category, gun caliber in both cases 20.3 cm).

To avoid long descriptions, the principal regulations are summarized in the table.

Principal Regulations			
Standard displacement	10,000–27,000 tons	up to 33,000 tons	Article IX
Number of ships	as many as possible within the total tonnage	two	Article IX
Armament	10 20.3 cm LAGs or unlimited no. of 15.2 cm LAGs + unlimited no. of HAGs to 12.7 cm	8 20.3 cm LAGs or unlimited no. of 15.2 cm LAGs + unlimited no. of HAGs to 12.7 cm	Article X
Age limit	20 years		
Replacement	Ships possessed on 12 November 1922 are trial constructions and may be replaced at once; otherwise, only after attaining the age limit. However, the keel of the replacement ship may not be laid earlier than 17 years after the completion of the aircraft carrier that will be replaced. In case of loss or accident the replacement ship may be built at once.		Article VIII; Chapter II, Part 3, Section I c)
Reconstruction	reinforcement of the protection against air and submarine attacks (bottom, torpedo bulges, horizontal armour) provided that the displacement does not increase more than 3,000 tons		Chapter II, Part 3, Section 1 d)

Note:
LAG = low-angle gun; HAG = high-angle gun

The Washington Arms Limitation Treaty contained quantitative and qualitative limitations for aircraft carriers but did not refer to *Hōshō*. She displaced less than 10,000 tons and was not to be added to the total tonnage corresponding to the definition of the aircraft carrier in the treaty. Japan was, therefore, permitted to build aircraft carriers within the total tonnage of 81,000 tons.

However, the situation was quite different in view of *Shōkaku* and the second, unnamed aircraft carrier. With performances not much better than those of *Hōshō*, these aircraft carriers would by no means respond to the individual fighting power of aircraft carriers permitted to be built within the treaty limits.

On the basis of this evaluation, both ships shared their fate with that of most ships of the Eight-Four Fleet, Eight-Six Fleet, and Eight-Eight Fleet Completion Programs then under construction or not yet laid down: they were canceled.

The Second Revision of the Imperial National Defense Policy

With the conclusion of the "Four-Power Treaty" (United States, Britain, Japan, and France) on December 13, 1921, during the Washington Conference, the Anglo-Japanese Alliance was dissolved. The end of this alliance[7] exerted great influence on the Japanese defense policy. Even though the "Nine-Power Treaty," and article XIX of the Washington Arms Limitation Treaty, decided the maintenance of the status quo, in view of the fortification of islands in the Pacific and the establishment of fleet bases at the time of the conclusion of the treaty, so that Japan could be sure not to be endangered by "new fortifications" of the United States on the Philippines, Guam, and the Aleutians, and of Britain at Hong Kong, the 5:5:3 ratio cemented the inferiority of Japan.[8] With the conclusion of the Washington Arms Limitation Treaty, the Imperial National Defense Policy had to be revised. The strategy had to be adapted to the drastically changed political situation abroad, and also at home, and the strength requirements had to consider the regulated quantitative possession.

The general staff and the naval general staff began negotiations about the revision in March 1922, and an agreement was reached on December 5, 1922. After it passed various military and political conferences, the second revision was sanctioned by the emperor on February 28, 1923.

As potential enemies the United States, Russia, and China were recognized, in that order. Britain had to be considered despite the opinion that hostilities with this nation could almost be excluded. Most probable was a clash with the United States, even though the limitations of the Washington Arms Limitation Treaty rendered the strategic offensive warfare for the US Navy more difficult and eliminated it for the IJN. Consequently, the defense should be directed to this hypothetical enemy. For this purpose, the "Military Strength Requirements" contained as a minimum necessary force nine capital ships, three aircraft carriers, twelve large ("Washington") cruisers,[9] and the corresponding number of auxiliary ships (40 cruisers, 16 flotilla leaders for destroyer and submarine squadrons, 144 destroyers, and 70 submarines).

The aircraft carriers were to be standard types of 27,000 tons each. As stated by the chief delegate and IJN minister Katō Tomosaburō at the Washington Conference, Japan wanted to take advantage of the maximum tonnage permitted by the treaty.

CHAPTER 2
The Standard Aircraft Carriers Akagi and Kaga

The Selection of Akagi and Kaga for Conversion

In conformity with Article IX of the Washington Treaty, the authorities selected the battle cruisers *Amagi* and *Akagi* for conversion into 27,000-ton aircraft carriers.[1] The construction of both ships had been permitted in the Eight-Eight Fleet Completion Program as battle cruisers No. 9 (*Amagi*) and No. 10 (*Akagi*).[2] During the design of this class, the weak point of the battle cruiser had been eliminated by adopting armor protection similar to the battleships of the Nagato class. The high speed was maintained by increasing engine power to 131,200 shaft horsepower (shp) and adopting a longer hull, despite the designed displacement of 41,200 tons. The main armament, ten 41 cm guns in five twin turrets, was identical to that of the battleships of the Kaga class. With this design, the thought of the later-realized high-speed battleship was adopted.

Amagi had been laid down on December 16, 1920, at Yokosuka Naval Arsenal, and *Akagi* at Kure Naval Arsenal on December 6, 1920; both ships were about 40 percent complete when the treaty was signed. On February 5, 1922, the day before signing the treaty, the Navy Ministry ordered construction work on the majority of major warships to be stopped, allowing work to continue on only eighteen ships, among them the two aircraft carriers. The final decision on their construction was not made, however, until after the ratification of the treaty on August 17, 1923.[3]

Both units were included in the New Shipbuilding Replenishment Program in Accordance with the Washington Treaty (*Washington Jōyaku niyoru Kantei Seizō Shin Hojū Keikaku*), together with other ships whose construction had been proposed in July 1922. This program passed the forty-sixth session of the Diet (December 27, 1922–March 27, 1923) in March 1923 and superseded all previous programs.

However, during the Great Kantō earthquake, which took place on September 1, 1923, *Amagi* was so severely damaged[4] that she was deleted from the warship register on April 14, 1924, and assigned for scrap on May 12, 1924.[5]

The battleship *Kaga*, designated no. 3 in the Eight-Eight Fleet Completion Program, was selected as her replacement. The Kaga class (*Kaga* and *Tosa*) was an expanded version of the Nagato class, with stronger armament and better protection. It was the first class with inclined side armor and concentration of armor protection on the vital area. Compared with *Amagi*, the length was shorter, engine performance was less, and the planned displacement, at 39,900 tons, was also a little less.

Kaga had been laid down on July 19, 1920, at Kawasaki Kōbe Shipyard and was launched on November 17, 1921. The building stop had also been ordered on February 5, 1922, as was the case with *Akagi* and *Amagi*, and the incomplete hull was transferred to the IJN on July 11, 1922, prior to being towed to Yokosuka Naval Arsenal.

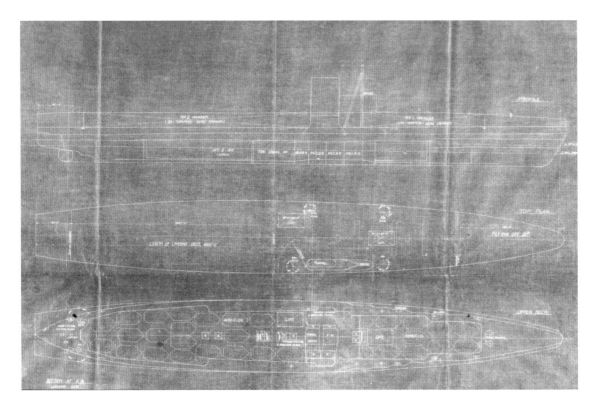

From December 1, 1920, to October 1, 1923, Captain / Rear Admiral Hiraga Yuzuru served as chief planner of the 4th Section of the Navy Technical Department and was responsible for the basic planning of the main ships of the Eight-Eight Fleet, and other IJN ships of the time. During this period, it was also decided to convert *Akagi* and *Kaga* into aircraft carriers in accordance with the Washington Disarmament Treaty. This and the following drawings show some of the trial-and-error examinations made by Hiraga and his colleagues. The first drawing shows *Kaga* (Project 2) with the superstructures to starboard, twelve 14 cm casemate guns on the main deck, two elevators, and about thirty-five airplanes. *Sekai no Kansen / Hiraga Yuzuru Dejitaru Ākaibu*

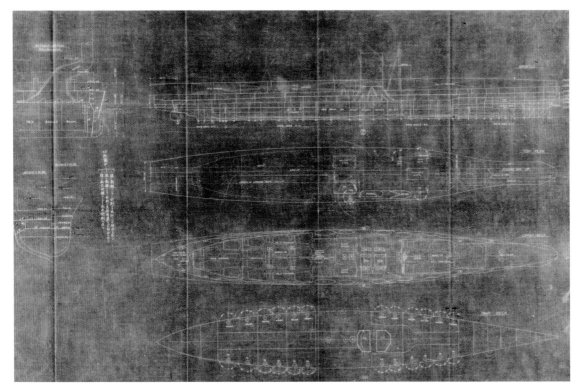

Kaga examination (Project 1 according to Hiraga) with upright funnel, narrowing flight deck forward, three elevators, the number of 14 cm casemate guns increased to twenty-four, and four 12 cm high-angle guns on the flight deck. Around thirty to forty airplanes, with about twenty-seven in the hangar. *Sekai no Kansen / Hiraga Yuzuru Dejitaru Ākaibu*

This *Amagi* and *Akagi* examination (Project 1) shows the proposed design with a full-length flight deck, the bridge structure on the starboard side, ten 50 cal. 20 cm guns and fourteen 45 cal. 12 cm single guns in casemates, and four 12 cm high-angle guns on the flight deck. *Sekai no Kansen / Hiraga Yuzuru Dejitaru Ākaibu*

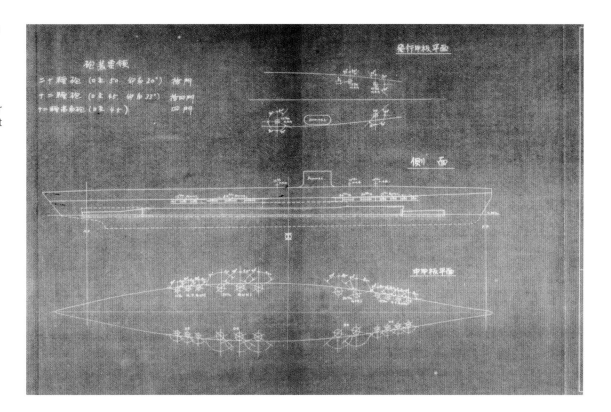

Amagi and *Akagi* as supersized aircraft carriers of approximately 27,000 tons. This study shows two flight decks, perhaps influenced by HMS *Furious*. The middle deck, where the 20 cm guns are located, is not connected to the hangar, and aircraft cannot be launched from it. The gun armament consists of two twin 20 cm gun turrets, six 20 cm casemate guns, six 12 cm casemate guns, and twelve 12 cm single high-angle guns. The funnel is bent outward, which differs from the actual completed version. *Sekai no Kansen / Hiraga Yuzuru Dejitaru Ākaibu*

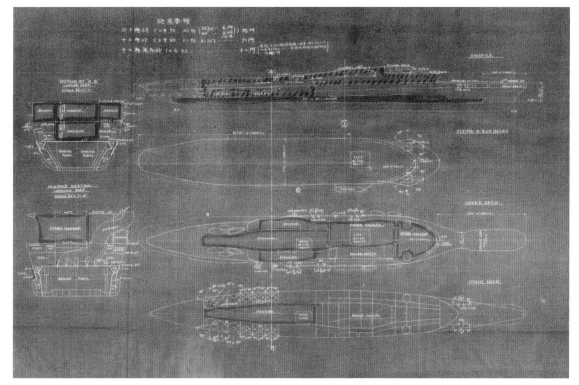

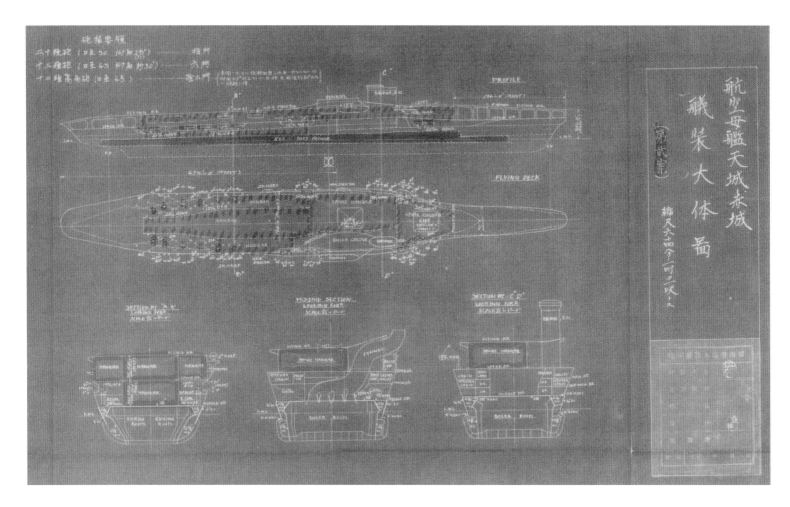

Amagi and *Akagi* study with single deck and tower-type bridge structure on the starboard side. Apart from the bent funnel, she looks like a larger version of the aircraft carrier *Hōshō*. The front part of the flight deck is very narrow and appears to be just the width of an airplane. The number of guns and other armament is the same as in the previous drawing (of the same date), but all the 20 cm guns are single casemate guns. The side armor is 152 mm, slightly thicker than *Akagi*'s actual side armor of 127 mm. *Sekai no Kansen / Hiraga Yuzuru Dejitaru Ākaibu*

Amagi and *Akagi* study with a low-silhouette, single-stage flight deck. The interior of the hangar depicts aircraft (biplanes) with wings folded, but it seems that only about thirty aircraft can be stored in the forward and aft hangars combined. The maximum number of aircraft carried on board may be forty to fifty at most. Although at first glance a modern design, even if the ship had been completed as it was, its aircraft-operating capacity would have been below par for the size of the hull, and it is highly likely that a major refit would have been required after all. *Sekai no Kansen / Hiraga Yuzuru Dejitaru Ākaibu*

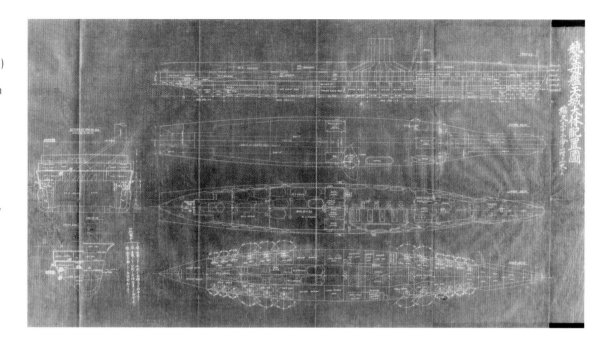

Another *Amagi* and *Akagi* study. A three-level flight deck ship with a funnel of the upward-sloping type. This study drawing is rather close to the actual *Akagi*. The hangars are also on three levels (upper, middle, and lower), and the number of aircraft on board seems to be around the actual sixty (including spares). The middle deck of *Akagi* was planned as a flight deck but is said to have lost its flight deck function when the 20 cm gun turrets and the compass bridge were placed there during the design process. A closer look at this study by Hiraga reveals that the compass bridge had already been placed on the middle deck, making the deck completely unusable as a flight deck. Since this drawing is also labeled "*Amagi*," it is thought to have been drawn before the Great Kantō earthquake. *Sekai no Kansen / Hiraga Yuzuru Dejitaru Ākaibu*

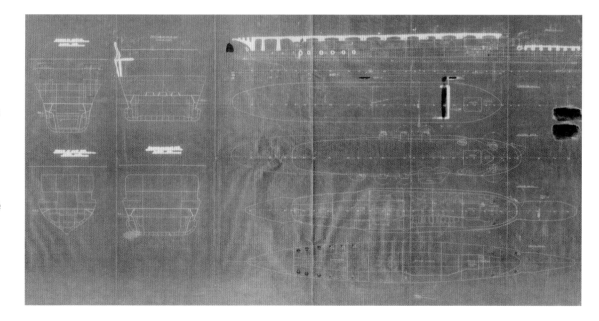

Akagi afloat on April 7, 1925. She had been launched at Kure Naval Arsenal (Kaigun Kōshō) on December 6, 1920, as a battle cruiser, but construction had to be halted as a result of the Washington Treaty. She remained afloat and her official launch date was changed to April 22, 1925. At the time of her conversion into an aircraft carrier, her hull was already considerably advanced, and it is said that the design changes and construction work were difficult. *Akagi*'s bow was not of the "spoon (*supūn*) type" used for the Nagato class, and the anchor deck largely remained as it was planned for the battle cruiser configuration.

As a result of the Washington Treaty, the hull of battle cruiser 9, *Amagi*, was selected to be converted into an aircraft carrier. She was about 40 percent complete when the treaty was signed, and according to Japanese press reports, work on her was resumed on January 19, 1923. Unfortunately, *Amagi* was badly damaged while under construction at Yokosuka Naval Arsenal (Kaigun Kōshō) as a result of the Great Kantō earthquake. This natural catastrophe hit the Kantō region on September 1, 1923, and *Amagi*'s stern slid off to the left of the slipway, and the hull became distorted. After investigation, the IJN decided that repairs and rebuilding would be too difficult, and *Amagi*'s hull was scrapped. She was replaced by the incomplete battleship *Kaga*. This photo shows *Amagi* on September 3–4, 1923, and was taken by Vice Admiral Matsumura Tatsuo.

所船造崎川戸神
Kawasaki Dock Kobe.

The battleship *Kaga* prior to launching at Kawasaki Kōbe Shipyard (Zōsensho). As can be seen, the ship has not yet received its side armor, and the wood backing (*bakkingu uddo*) looks almost white. The ship was launched with her stern facing south from building slip no. 4. Since *Kaga* was laid down as a battleship, she was named after a Japanese province, and Kaga is the former name of the southern part of the Ishikawa Prefecture. *Courtesy of Takagi Hiroshi*

Kaga was successfully launched after 08:30 on November 17, 1921, in the presence of some 100,000 visitors. The launching ceremony was held in honor of His Imperial Highness Prince Fushimi Hiroyasu (Fushiminomiya Hiroyasu). In this photo the large decorative ball (*kusudama*) is floating, with its five-colored paper pieces, in the autumn breeze. *Courtesy of Takagi Hiroshi*

Conversion of Akagi and Kaga

In the meantime, a design team in the Navy Technical Department under the direction of Commander (shipbuilding) Fujimoto Kikuo, the head of the Basic Design Section, had worked out the conversion plans, and the Navy Ministry issued the conversion orders for *Akagi* and *Kaga* on November 19, 1923. Two days later they were added to the aircraft carrier register, after *Wakamiya* (April 1, 1920), *Shōkaku* (March 3, 1921), and *Hōshō* (October 13, 1921).

Work on *Akagi* was resumed by Kure Naval Arsenal on November 9, 1923; that is, a few days before the official order. Simultaneously with her construction, the building dock was increased. With a length of 270 m, a width of 35 m, and a depth of 15 m, it had been possible to build *Akagi* without increasing the dimensions. However, in view of the tendency toward always larger ships, this work should have been executed at the same time. The lengthening to 335 m and the widening to 43 m influenced the tempo of *Akagi*'s conversion and also caused some problems for Commander (constructor) Suzuki Kakuji, in charge of both works. *Akagi* was therefore launched only on April 22, 1925. At that time, she was complete to the upper hangar only. The flight deck would be fitted only after floating to keep the draft as small as possible. The launching (floating) caused no problem—except for the music band. Even though the hull was already afloat in the dock, it took twenty-two minutes to bring it out from the dock. During this time, the band had to play the same piece again and again.

The work also proceeded slowly after the launching. Besides the particular fittings and equipment of an aircraft carrier, which were by no means definite but still in a more or less experimental stage, there were also financial problems. At the planning of the conversion, the IJN lacked experience, and the expenses became much higher than expected. The budget was already consumed after the completion of the hull and the usual fitting-out work. Higher expenses had been expected, such as for the equipment for flight operations, but the IJN, in view of the condition of the national finances, had stated conversion expenses that were lower than calculated in the budget and was now forced to use building expenses intended for other ships (such as *Kaga*) and repair costs to complete the conversion. This concealment continued after the official completion on March 25, 1927. Even though the ensign had been hoisted and the ship was assigned to the fleet, she remained at the fitting-out quay.[6] The equipment for flight operations was fitted one after another, and in May the tests of

the arrester gear and the elevators were finished. The work on the propulsion system was also completed, and before the official trials the bottom had to be cleaned and repainted. *Akagi* entered the fourth dock of Yokosuka Naval Arsenal on May 29 and returned to Kure on June 13 after finishing this work. Both cruises were recognized as trials, so the crew was on board. On June 17 and from June 21 to 24, trials were again run in the Inland Sea (Iyonada), with Beppu Bay as the base, and between these dates, test firing of the guns was carried out. After repeated work on the equipment for flight operations, takeoff and landing trials took place in the Iyonada on July 31, and also the official trial run was executed.

Conversion work on *Kaga* officially began on December 13, 1923, but the hull was not, in fact, converted until 1925, since Yokosuka Naval Arsenal had been damaged by the Great Kantō earthquake, and her conversion to a battleship of different dimensions from *Akagi* and *Amagi* necessitated another design. Actually, *Akagi* and *Kaga* were built to two different designs, and this required time. The official commissioning on March 31, 1928, marked the actual commencement of the fitting of equipment for flight operations and the trials, which lasted until she was assigned to the Combined Fleet on November 30, 1929.

The progress of the conversion work on *Kaga* was still slower than in the case of *Akagi*, because approximately 30 percent of her budget was used for the completion of *Akagi*. For the person in the yard who was mainly responsible, Captain (constructor) Nakagawa Susumu, one of the greatest difficulties was to secure finances, and he was in close connection with the man in charge of the budget in the Navy Technical Department.[7] Even though the ensign had been hoisted, the conversion was by no means complete at the official date, as stated above. Besides the equipment for flight operations, the crew spaces forward and aft were still incomplete, and tables, stools, wardrobes, etc. were piled up everywhere; electric cables were lacking in some places; paintwork was not completed; and all through the ship there were works waiting to be finished. Only one-third of the planned complement was on board. In contrast, the propulsion system, for which only uptakes and funnels had had to be revised, was completed, so *Kaga* could participate in the naval review on December 4, 1928, irrespective of the fact that she was incomplete as an aircraft carrier. After that, *Kaga* was moved to Sasebo Naval Arsenal on December 28 for some final fitting-out work.

Because the foregoing outline may give the impression that the IJN was rather lazy in the conversion of these ships, it must be pointed out that until this time, Japan's experience in building aircraft carriers was limited to the construction of the small *Hōshō*, which was no conversion but a newly built ship. The conversion of a battle cruiser and a battleship under construction into aircraft carriers, of more than three times the size of *Hōshō*, caused serious difficulties. These problems concerned design as well as reconstruction. For instance, prior to conversion, *Akagi* was complete as far as the armor deck. This deck had to be lowered by one deck, and its thickness reduced generally from 96 mm to 79 mm, and even 57 mm over the area between the belt armor and the longitudinal torpedo bulkhead. Therefore, the upper part of the torpedo bulge and the height of the belt armor and its support had to be altered, because the draft as a battle cruiser differed from that as an aircraft carrier. The thickness of the side armor plates, which had already been manufactured, was reduced from 254 mm to 152 mm by rerolling.[8]

In the case of *Kaga*, the armor deck remained at the original height—mainly for financial reasons. In order to obtain the quite necessary lowering of the center of gravity, the thickness had to be reduced to 38 mm from 102 mm. On the other hand, the change of the position of the bulge was not necessary, because the position of the armor deck remained the same. However, following the lower edge of the belt armor, the upper part of the bulge, inclined outward, was armored by 127 mm thick armor. It was, besides increasing the protection, also a measure to lower the center of gravity. The thickness of the belt armor was reduced from 280 mm to 152 mm, as on *Akagi*.[9]

Even though the hull was left, in principle,[10] as initially designed below the armor deck, the ship above this deck was in fact completely reconstructed. In addition, beam had to be reduced compared with the original design, in order to regulate metacentric height and also to reduce weight.

At this time, aircraft technology had progressed rapidly, but war experience was sparse—and what was known by the navies that had participated in World War I was not fully made available to others. For these reasons, unique aircraft carriers evolved, incorporating conclusions that were based on investigations of the British seaplane tenders and aircraft carriers and on original ideas in layout and shape of the flight decks, funnel arrangement, and gun armament. However, this unique design did not prove successful, and a substantial reconstruction became necessary.

Comparison of the Main Armor Thicknesses (in mm) of Akagi and Kaga in the Configurations of Battle Cruiser / Battleship and Aircraft Carrier				
Ship	**Akagi**		**Kaga**	
Armor location / configuration	BC	CV	BB	CV
Belt armor, central part	254 VC	152 VC*	280 VC	152 VC
fore and after parts	228 VC	152 VC*	254 VC	127 VC**
Horizontal armor, armor deck	96 NVNC		102 NVNC	
middle deck, flat part	22–46 HT	79 NVNC* (lower deck)	38–63 HT	38 NVNC (middle deck)
middle deck, inclined parts	70 HT		63–76 HT	
lower deck, above ER + BR	22 HT		25–19 HT	
LTB	73 HT	73 HT	76 HT	76 HT
Splinter bulkhead behind LTB	13–19 HT	38 HT	13–19 HT	19 HT

Notes:
BC = battle cruiser; BB = battleship; CV = aircraft carrier; VC = Vickers cemented; NVNC = New Vickers non cemented; HT = high tensile (steel); ER = engine room; BR = boiler room; LTB = longitudinal torpedo bulkhead.
* 152 mm in original plans but actually 127 mm (*Sekai no Kansen*, no. 944, pp. 99–100), assumed to be the same for *Kaga*.
** There are also sources stating 90 mm. The data in the table are taken from drawings obtained from the National Archives, Washington, and they are considered reliable.

Akagi pictured on her naming ceremony on April 22, 1925, at Kure Naval Arsenal. This photo was taken by engineer Yagi Sugi, and we can see that the large ball (*kusudama*) has been broken, and that pigeons and five-colored pieces of paper are scattered by the air from the compressed air pipe. The ball was broken by the arsenal's director, Rear Admiral Godō Takuo, and the naming ceremony was rather simple. Shortly after the ceremony, work continued, but since Kure's no. 4 dock was unfinished, the final work had to be carried out in no. 5 dock at Yokosuka Kaigun Kōshō. *Akagi* (Red Castle) was laid down as a battle cruiser and was therefore named after a mountain. Mount Akagi (Akagi-yama) is located in the Gunma Prefecture.

Commemorative assembly at the naming ceremony of *Akagi*, taken by Captain Nagamura Kiyoshi's camera in the Shipbuilding Department of Kure Naval Arsenal on April 22, 1925. The photo shows the main responsible individuals for *Akagi*'s conversion. *Sitting, from left:* Rear Admiral (constructor) Suzuki Keiji and Rear Admiral (constructor) Hiraga Yuzuru. *Standing, from left:* Commander (constructor) Suzuki Kakuji, Captain (constructor) Nagamura Kiyoshi, Commander (constructor) Fujimoto Kikuo, Rear Admiral (paymaster) Nakano Shigaharu, Captain (constructor) Kubo Tsunahiko, and engineer Yokota Eikichi.

In accordance with Article IX of the Washington Arms Limitation Treaty, the IJN chose the battle cruisers *Amagi* and *Akagi* for conversion into aircraft carriers. However, *Amagi* was irreparably damaged on the slip by the Great Kantō earthquake on September 1, 1923. Lacking another incomplete battle cruiser, the IJN selected the battleship *Kaga*, the no. 3 battleship of the Eight-Eight Fleet, as replacement, irrespective of her lesser suitability (shorter length and lower speed). In addition, her selection necessitated a substantial revision of the design. In other words, instead of using one design for the conversions, the designers were practically forced to make two designs. Note the huge support posts for the upper flight deck, and the large rectangular openings of the casemates. Since there were budget restrictions, a considerable number of workers from Asano Shipyard and other builders were used. Note the mast of the coast defense ship *Yakumo* in the background.

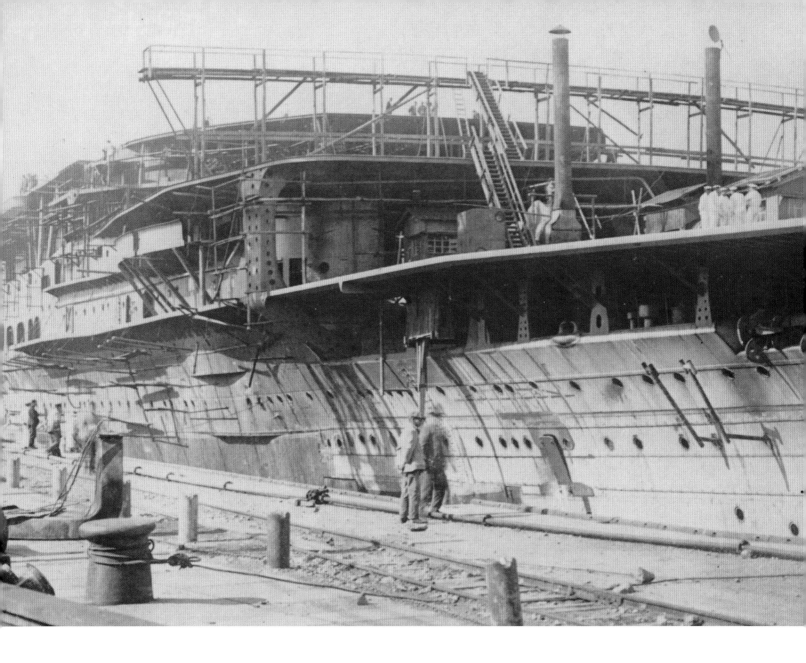

Kaga during fitting-out on February 20, 1928. Here *Kaga* is docked in no. 5 dock at Yokosuka Naval Arsenal. The lower flight deck is protruding from the just above the forecastle deck. Note the second anchor lashed to the anchor bed, as on older warships.

CHAPTER 3
Outline Description of Akagi

Flight Decks, Hangars, Elevators, and Avgas Tanks

A new and characteristic feature was the three-stage flight deck. The upper deck,[1] 190.20 m long and 30.48 m wide, was designed as a takeoff-and-landing deck. Over 40 percent of its length sloped down toward the bow, while the after 60 percent was inclined 1.5° toward the stern relative to the waterline, the intention being to achieve a favorable airflow over the deck for landing aircraft and to support the slowing down of their speed. The middle flight deck, which began immediately forward on the "bridge," was only 15 m long and hence was so short that the smallest aircraft must have had problems in taking off. Two fighters should have been able to take off from that deck in case of urgency, but, as will be stated later, this deck was never used operationally. The lower flight deck was 55.02 m long by 22.86 m wide and was intended as the takeoff deck for the larger torpedo aircraft. Although this deck was very short by today's standards, it was adequate for the slow, lightweight aircraft of the time. In fact, it was used later as the takeoff deck for fighters, which normally would have used the middle deck.

This arrangement was intended to facilitate simultaneous takeoff and landing without obstructions,[2] as well as allowing the rapid takeoff of aircraft directly from the hangar, without the need to transport the planes via an elevator. However, the advantages that the IJN had hoped to obtain with this design eventually became disadvantages due to the enormous strides in aircraft development made subsequently. With ever heavier planes of higher and higher speed requiring ever-longer takeoff and landing distances, the three-stage flight deck completely lost its raison d'être. The upper flight deck was too short for the simultaneous takeoff and landing of planes and also did not permit planes to be carried on it, such as in the case of the aircraft carriers of the United States Navy (USN). Therefore, the aircraft capacity was small in relation to the size of the ships and if compared with the aircraft carriers USS *Lexington* and *Saratoga* of the USN.

No other navy can show examples of this arrangement, the only ships in any way comparable being the British aircraft carriers *Furious*, *Courageous*, and *Glorious*, especially the former. The two-level arrangement of these aircraft carriers served as a model for *Akagi* and *Kaga*, with the addition of the middle stage for the takeoff of small aircraft to further improve the fighting power.

Longitudinal arrester gear, of British design, was adopted for the braking and guidance of landing aircraft because Japanese constructors had not yet been able to develop a domestic system.

A further indication that the British aircraft carriers were taken as models was the step in the upper flight deck of *Akagi*, by which the deviation of the landing plane to the side of the flight deck should be prevented. The profile of the deck and its position to the waterline are shown in the figure.[3]

Hangars were provided on three levels aft (about from the position of the bridge, after conversion, and aft) and two levels forward. The upper hangar was placed directly below the takeoff-and-landing deck. It was of the open type,[4] and strong supports were needed at both sides to carry the flight deck. It was designated "wartime hangar" (*senji kakunōka*) and was connected with the middle takeoff deck; that is, from it the fighters should have been able to make a rapid takeoff.

The hangar below was connected to the lower flight deck and was of the closed type, as was the lowermost hangar in the aft half of the hull. The latter was used in peacetime for reserve aircraft parts.

The total capacity of the hangars was sixty aircraft (sixteen type 3 fighters, twenty-eight type 13 torpedo bombers, and sixteen type 10 reconnaissance planes)—a remarkably small number considering the size of the vessel.

One aircraft elevator was fitted forward and one aft. The forward one (measuring 11.8 m × 13.0 m) was offset to starboard and was used for transport of the larger planes, while the aft one (12.8 m × 8.4 m) was intended to handle the smaller aircraft.

Because *Akagi* and *Kaga* were designed as "flush deck" aircraft carriers,[5] the "bridge" was situated below the flight deck, at the forward end of the upper hangar. It was first planned to place this command center only to port and to fit a simple observation station to starboard. However, this arrangement was found to be unfavorable for steering, and in recognition of the opinion of the fitting-out personnel, a large ship's command center was fitted at the place stated above, stretching over the whole beam. As a result, the forward part of the upper hangar was closed and the middle takeoff deck could no longer be used. In addition, the twin 20 cm turrets fitted on each side of the midlevel flight deck formed another hindrance.

Before the "bridge" type was decided on, the yard produced a real-size mockup, and *Akagi*'s bridge was built only after repeated tests.

Something new was the manhole-like windows in the ceiling (the upper flight deck) to have visual connection with this takeoff-and-landing deck.

As in the case of *Hōshō*'s bridge, after conversion, there were platforms at each side projecting over the beam of the upper flight deck, for observation of flight operations and airspace and also ease of navigation.

The signal mast and the wireless masts placed on both sides were lowered during flight operations. On the basis of the experiences with *Hōshō*, great care was taken that no equipment projected over the takeoff-and-landing deck during flight operations.

The construction of the aviation gasoline (avgas) tanks provided a particular problem. This almost "deadly danger" in case of an explosion had already been recognized during the construction of *Hōshō*, but research on the best method began only when the large aircraft carriers were constructed, which had to carry considerably larger amounts of this liquid. To find out the most favorable structure, tightness and damage control, an investigation committee was established in Kure Naval Arsenal, and several models of tanks of different structure were produced. They were filled with avgas, exploded at Kamegakubi range, and subsequently investigated. On the basis of these experiments, the construction method of the tanks (structural strength, division, arrangement of pumps and pipes, sealing, etc.) was decided. However, further tests were carried out in 1930 and resulted in revisions to the entire avgas supply system.[6]

Fitting of a windscreen (or windbreak) on the flight deck of *Akagi* in 1926. The windscreen was composed of several sections that were raised or lowered by a mechanical-hydraulic system fitted on the flight deck. Note the large number of longitudinal wires of the British-type arrester gear, initially fitted on both *Akagi* and *Kaga*. The retardation power proved to be insufficient. The bow of the ship is to the right.

Portside view of *Akagi* when cruising in the Western Inland Sea on October 7, 1926, when being prepared for trials. Because dock no. 4 at Kure Naval Arsenal was not yet completed, *Akagi* had to sail to Yokosuka Naval Arsenal in October. She entered dock no. 5 and had her bottom cleaned and painted. Note the open upper hangar, called the wartime hangar (*senji kakunōko*). It was the only example of a completely open hangar in the Imperial Japanese Navy, and it was to disappear when *Akagi* was rebuilt. The reason for installing this type of hangar was to keep the displacement below 27,000 tons, because in this case the treaty permitted the mounting of ten 20 cm guns (instead of eight), but they are not yet mounted. If necessary, the sides and front of the hangar could be closed by canvas. The ceiling height within the upper hangar was about 5 m. Smoke from the small upward-directed funnel shows that the eight mixed-burning boilers are in operation.

Type 10 carrier-based fighters are being prepared to take off from the lower flight deck of *Akagi* in the autumn of 1927. In March 1927, the aircraft carrier *Hōshō* joined the fleet as attached to the Combined Fleet (*Rengō Kantai*), followed in August of the same year by the giant *Akagi*. Thus, the two aircraft carriers were used during major exercises in September and October of the same year, and many lessons were learned. The planes shown are outside the hangar, and it seems as if the short flight deck was long enough for the slow, lightweight aircraft of the time. This and the other flight decks were covered with 63.5 mm wide and 38.1 mm thick boards made of American teak. *Kure Maritime Museum*

A type 10 fighter is launched from the lower flight deck of *Akagi* in the autumn of 1927. The white lines that radiate from the tip of the bow were used to determine the direction of the wind by blowing steam. The forward edge of the deck was less than 10 m above the waterline. At first glance, the multistage flight deck appeared to be very advantageous, since it enabled the ship to launch and land planes at the same time, but in reality the short flight decks were rarely practical, and only the upper flight deck was used. *Maru Special*

Type 14-2 reconnaissance seaplanes aboard *Akagi*. The planes were stored on trolleys on the short boat deck below the aft end of the flight deck. Note the shape of the flight deck stanchions. The portside one has a truss structure, while the starboard one has a box structure with holes. *Maru Special*

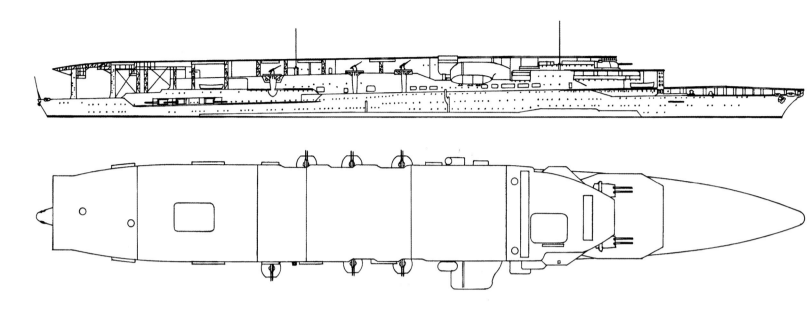

Profile and plan of *Akagi* in 1929. *Sekai no Kansen*

A starboard view of *Akagi* taken in the autumn of 1930. This photo shows the three-stage flight deck, of which only the uppermost was a true flight deck for takeoff and landing of aircraft. The middle flight deck (*chūdan hikō kanpan*) was intended to be used for the takeoff of fighters from the "wartime hangar," but it could not be used because of the two 20 cm twin turrets (said to have been mounted in 1929). This deck was therefore called the turret deck (*hōtō kanpan*). The lower flight deck (55.02 m long and 22.86 m wide) was connected to the middle hangar, and it was planned that bombers could take off directly from this hangar deck. Note the funnels, the guns, and the huge posts supporting the aft part of the flight deck.

Akagi with a full load of airplanes photographed in Ōsaka Bay on October 15, 1934 (estimated). The photo shows a large number of type 13 attack planes (*kankō*), and maintenance personnel are moving planes with folded wings to the launching positions. The windscreen is raised and the planes are marked with the katakana character "ha" (ハ) for *Akagi*. Since early 1934, *Akagi* had been fitted with the Kure-type model 2 transverse arrester gear. Note the zebra-like marking (red and white) on the curved shape of the aft end of the flight deck. This photo was taken by the *Ōsaka Mainichi Shimbun*, and it was naturally banned by the IJN. Also note the flag of Rear Admiral Katagiri Eikichi, commander of the 2nd Carrier Division.

Aerial view of *Akagi* and the battleship *Nagato* at Yokosuka Naval Arsenal on August 15, 1930. Note the difference in size between the 261.2 m long *Akagi* and the 215.8 m long *Nagato*. Until the completion of the battleship *Yamato*, *Akagi* was the Navy's longest ship. The forward elevator is in the down position, and also visible are two windscreens forward and aft of the elevator. The upper flight deck was slightly to port to offset the weight of the funnels. In 1931 *Akagi* was fitted with the Fieux transverse cable system, and in 1933 this system was superseded by the Kayaba system, which in early 1934 was superseded by the Kure-type model 2. Part of dock no. 5 is slightly visible in the upper right-hand corner of the image.

A rare portside view of *Akagi* in Yokosuka taken in 1931–33 by Hatakeyama Satarō. She is moored at naval port no. 3 (*gunkō dai 3*), and the anchor chain is fixed to a buoy. When the particulars for the main anchors and chains were being decided, the data from the huge passenger liners (40,000–60,000 gross tons) operating on the Atlantic route were evaluated.

Portside view of *Akagi* taken at Yokosuka in 1934–35. Most noteworthy is the small tower-type bridge to starboard on the forward part of the flight deck. This bridge was fitted at Yokosuka Naval Arsenal between December 1933 and January 1934. From that time, the compass bridge, situated at the forward edge of the flight deck, was used as a control station for takeoff and landing of planes. This was a public photo and consequently considerably modified, as can be seen when looking at the waterline. *Kure Maritime Museum*

Propulsion System

The propulsion system consisted of the original four Gihon turbine sets planned for the ship as a battle cruiser. Each set consisted of two high-pressure and two low-pressure turbines geared to a single shaft via four pinions. The cruising turbines were connected in parallel to the high-pressure turbines and in series to the low-pressure turbines. Designed performance was 131,200 shp on four shafts, to give the ship a speed of 30 knots at 210 rpm. The turbines weighed 311 tons and the gears 272 tons, totaling 583 tons. The power/weight ratio was 224 shp/ton.

The steam for the operation of the turbines was supplied by nineteen Kampon type B (*Otsu*) boilers. Eleven were oil burners, and eight were mixed burners.

At the trial run on June 17, 1927, *Akagi* attained 32.5 knots, even though only 28.5 knots were officially stated. On June 24, 32.6 knots, with 137,000 shp and 214 rpm of the shafts, was attained. The increase in the speed was primarily caused by the reduction of the original normal displacement of 41,200 tons to a 34,364-tonne trial displacement by the conversion—the same machinery naturally produced a higher speed in a lighter vessel. The 3,900 tons of oil and 2,100 tons of coal, totaling 6,000 tons of liquid and solid fuel, gave a designed range of 8,000 miles at 14 knots.

One of the greatest design problems of the conversion was how to arrange uptakes and funnels. The swiveling funnels of *Hōshō* had not proved ideal, since the smoke often steamed across the flight deck. The hot gases caused air turbulence, and at times the disturbances were so severe that no aircraft could land.

Consequently, a 1/48-scale model of *Akagi* was constructed, with a scale volume of 1:110,600, which underwent extensive testing in the wind tunnel of the Navy Technical Research Institute (*Kaigun Gijutsu Kenkyushō*) at Kasumigaura before the conversion. No suitable solution was found, and as a result the authorities agreed on one large funnel situated at about 40 percent of the length and projecting obliquely to starboard, just below the upper flight deck and cranked through at an angle of approximately 120°, so that its mouth pointed downward at about this angle, plus one small funnel fitted immediately abaft it and led vertically slightly over the takeoff-and-landing deck. To accommodate this funnel arrangement, this deck was offset to port, and consequently the shape of the sponsons for the 12 cm high-angle guns varied.

The large funnel was connected with the uptakes of the forward eleven oil-burning boilers. The small funnel was used for the usual cruising navigation and was not in operation when aircraft took off or landed; it was for the exhaust of the eight mixed-fuel-burning boilers.

The upper rear section of the larger funnel's casing (facing upward and to port) was fitted with an opening sealed with a blind cover. This was a safety measure in case damage caused a severe list. If the mouth of the funnel reached the surface of the water, the cover could be removed by actuating the corresponding system, allowing the exhaust gases to escape through this opening. To avoid, or at least reduce, the turbulences caused by the hot exhaust gases, a cooling system was fitted by which sea water was sprinkled into the funnel to reduce the temperature and press the smoke in the direction of the water surface.[7]

Main reduction gear of *Akagi*.
Courtesy of Takagi Hiroshi

Principal plan of *Akagi*'s machinery structure. *Courtesy of Takagi Hiroshi*

Key:
(1) Figure 140 (B): Rough plan of the aircraft carrier *Akagi*'s main machinery structure
(2) Low-pressure (turbine)
(3) Astern steam inlet
(4) Astern nozzle valve
(5) Auxiliary exhaust (steam) inlet
(6) Exhaust (steam) outlet
(7) Dog clutch
(8) Main reduction gear
(9) Steam reservoir pipe
(10) High-pressure (turbine)
(11) Main steam inlet
(12) Drainpipe-fixing seat

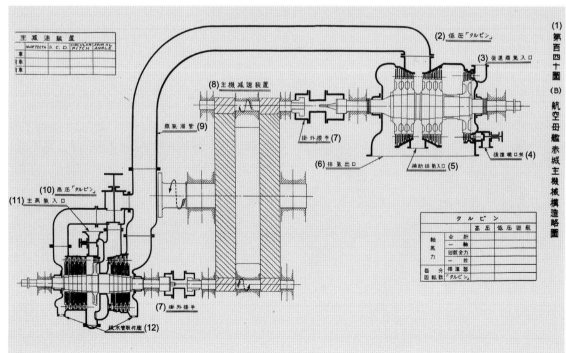

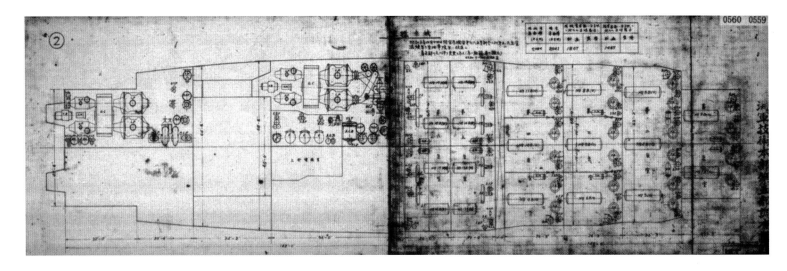

General arrangement of the propulsion plant of *Akagi* (surveyed November 2, 1932). *Sekai no Kansen*

Akagi steaming in the Inland Sea on June 17, 1927, in preparation for the full-load trials. Note that smoke is emitted from both funnels and shows that the eleven pure heavy oil-burning boilers are also in operation. It is said that the mixed-burning boilers were not used when the ship launched and landed aircraft, since the smoke could have a negative impact. This means that the ship could not sail at full power during air operations, something that may have limited the maximum number of aircraft that could be launched. White smoke is emitted from the forward funnel, showing that the hot-smoke-cooling system (seawater spray system) is in operation. *Akagi*'s propulsion system was the same as for the planned battle cruiser configuration: four Gihon geared-turbine sets (two HPTs and two LPTs connected to one shaft by four pinions, the CRTs connected in parallel to the HPTs and in series to the LPTs), designed for 131,000 shp on four shafts (propeller diameter 4.572 m) and 30 knots with 210 rpm. The steam for operation of turbines was generated by nineteen boilers: eleven oil burners and eight mixed burners. On June 17, *Akagi* attained 32.5 knots (officially 28.5 knots); on June 24 she attained 32.6 knots with 137,000 shp and 214 rpm. The main reason for the increased speed was the reduction of the displacement from 41,200 tons to 34,364 tons.

Armament

Akagi's standard displacement was officially reported as 26,000 tons but was, in fact, about 29,500 tons. The official data allowed for the installation of ten 8-inch (20.32 cm) guns, as compared with the eight aboard her US rivals *Saratoga* and *Lexington*. One twin turret was located on each side of the middle flight deck in front of the bridge, by which this deck was termed "gun turret deck," and three single mountings in casemates along each side aft. In addition, the mounting of three 12 cm low-angle guns in casemates on each side and their replacement by 20 cm guns in the event of war had been planned, but this idea fortunately was abandoned. The IJN had aimed at providing superiority in firepower, but the adopted arrangement actually placed her at a disadvantage compared with the US aircraft carriers. The superimposed arrangement of twin turrets fore and aft of the island bridge allowed all eight guns to fire on the broadside, while the maximum broadside on *Akagi* was five guns. It must also be considered that the casemate guns could not always be used due to their low position, and their arc of fire was furthermore remarkably restricted.

The installation of 20 cm guns in casemates was unique in the IJN and was the largest caliber that could be mounted in this kind of carriage. Until then, the secondary armament of battleships and battle cruisers had always consisted of 14 or 15.2 cm guns. The gun was the 50 cal. 20 cm Mod 3 No. 1, which had a caliber of 200 mm and also formed the main armament of the heavy cruisers of the Furutaka, Aoba, and Myōkō classes before their conversion. The reasoning behind fitting this gun in an aircraft carrier was that it might be engaged in an artillery fight with a heavy cruiser.

At that time, the fitting of low-angle guns was considered to be an important component of the ship's fighting power. In fact, such an armament for an aircraft carrier was completely illogical because the vulnerability of the flight installations (hangars, flight deck, avgas storage, and supply system) did not permit it to fight a gun battle. Nevertheless, virtually all Japanese authors stress that this armament was an impressive feature. In reality it was inappropriate, reflecting the uncertainty prevailing at that time about the use and design features of the aircraft carrier; further examples are the three-stage flight deck and the funnel arrangement. However, it must be admitted that such armaments had some origin in the political and even psychological effects of the Washington Treaty, a fact that is also reflected by the 20.3 cm armament of the US aircraft carriers.

There were two main gun command stations, one to port and one to starboard, placed aft of the bridge and just below the upper flight deck. Each station was equipped with one type 13 fire director (*hōiban*). Two 4.5 m rangefinders, one on each side, were fitted on the auxiliary firing-command stations (one deck below and aft of the main gun command stations).

Six twin 12 cm high-angle guns were situated on sponsons amidships, three at each side. The position was very low and did not permit them to fire on aircraft attacking from the opposite side. Aside from the number, which was very small for the size of the ship, their position was also a remarkable disadvantage.

Generally, it was not until the strategic and tactical requirements of the aircraft carrier were harmonized, and the technical problems were overcome, that a basis for design was developed that took account of the aircraft carriers' special features and operational principles. Even then this could not be exploited immediately for political (Washington and London treaties) and budgetary reasons. The gap between requirements and technical solutions led to an extensive conversion some years after completion, during which the external appearance of both aircraft carriers was completely altered, bringing them in line with modern aircraft carrier configuration.

Comparison between the 50 Cal. 3-Year Type 20 cm Gun and the No. 2 20 cm Gun

Gun	(No. 1) 20 cm gun	No. 2 20 cm gun
Actual bore (mm)	200.0	203.2
Length oa (m)	10.310	10.310
Length (m)	10.000	10.000
Bore length (cal.)	50.00	49.21
Barrel weight with breech (t)	17.900	17.882
Max. bore pressure (normal service charge) (kg/mm^2)	30.0	30.0
Rifling	uniform right	uniform right
Number of grooves	48	48
Charge weight (70C2) (kg)	32.630	33.800
Number of powder bags	2	2
Muzzle velocity (m/s)	870	835

Source:
Tsutsumi Akio, *Sekai no Kansen*, no. 944, p. 113.

Comparison of the Shells of the 50 Cal 4-Year Type 20 cm Gun and the No. 2 20 cm Gun

Gun	(No 1) 20 cm gun		No 2 20 cm gun	
Shell	Type 88 AP shell	common shell	Type 91 AP shell	Type 91 common shell
Shell weight (kg)	110.00	110.00	125.85	125.85
Shell diameter (mm)	199.91	199.91	202.3	202.3
Shell length (mm)	762	769	906.2	888.0
Fuze	Type 13 No. 4	Type 91 time fuze	Type 13 No 4	Type 91 time fuze
Explosive	Shimose Type 91	Shimose	Shimose Type 91	Shimose
Explosive weight (kg)	2.836	8.144	3.100	8.140
Total length of guiding rings* (mm)	65	65	65	65
Maximum diameter of guiding rings* (mm)	211.2	211.2	214.96	214.96

Source:
Tsutsumi Akio, *Sekai no Kansen*, no. 944: 114.

Note:
* Also called driving bands (*dōkan*)

A photo of *Akagi* looking up from starboard aft, estimated to have been taken around 1930–31. This photograph is quite rare since it captures the details of the aft flight deck pillars very clearly. It is very interesting to note that the shape of each support pillar differs from the next, but it could be said that this is a complication unique to converted aircraft carriers. At this time, aircraft carriers were also seaplane carriers. The cavity in front of the pillars leads to the rear of the middle hangar, which was used for loading and unloading seaplanes (*suijōki*) from the stern. Note the single 20 cm guns in casemates, the 12 cm twin high-angle guns, and the starboard-side construction. It is reported that toward the end of her three-deck configuration, *Akagi* was fitted with ten 13 mm machine guns.

Akagi photographed outside Kōbe during the naval review on October 26, 1930. Note the low positions of the sponsons for the three twin 12 cm high-angle guns. The positions would not be changed during the later reconstruction, and this substantially reduced the effectiveness of the ship's antiaircraft gunnery. Note the four raised 110 cm retractable searchlights on the flight deck.

This photo can be compared with a previous photo in this book, in which *Akagi* is shown at an angle very similar to this one. Note that in this photo, the three starboard-side twin 12 cm high-angle mounts have been covered with shields, whereas in the previous photo they are covered only with canvas. The shields protected the mounts and the crew from the soot and smoke from the funnels. *Akagi*'s soot shields (*baien yoke*) were installed at the Yokosuka Naval Arsenal from May 10 to May 23, 1931. Since this photo was published in a public publication in November 1932, it can be determined that the photo was taken between May 1931 and October 1932. The sharp shape of the stern with a large overhang was characteristic of this ship, which had been converted from an unfinished battle cruiser, and was clearly different from *Kaga*, which had been converted from an unfinished battleship. The shooting location seems to be Yokosuka, the port where she was registered. *Sekai no Kansen*

Protection

The side, horizontal, and underwater protection of the original design was taken over virtually unchanged, with the exception of the reduction in belt thickness and the lowering of the armor deck, which have already been mentioned. The principle was to obtain protection against 20.3 cm shells, to be capable of fighting an enemy heavy cruiser. The distribution of the armor is shown in the amidships section drawing.

Ship's Boats

The majority of the ship's boats (*tantei*) were motorboats (*naikatei*), and they were stored on the upper deck, aft of the aft end of the middle hangar and below the flight deck. Cranes were mounted on the aft heavy supports of the flight deck, by which the boats could be lowered and heaved.

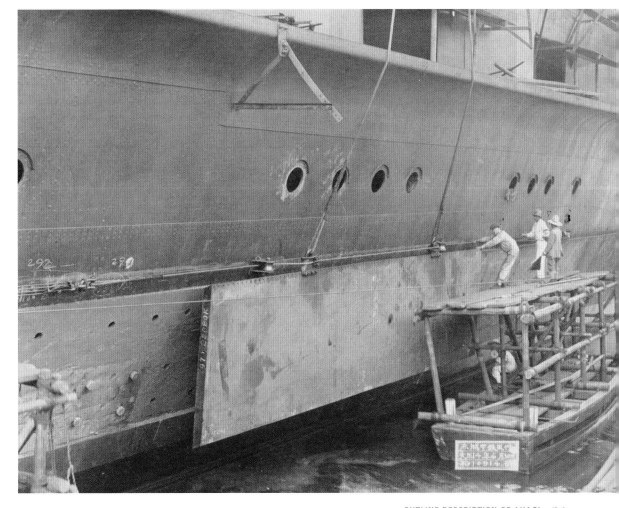

The redesigning of the 41,000-ton battle cruiser *Akagi* into a 26,900-ton aircraft carrier was very difficult, as was the conversion of the incomplete hull. This photo from June 30, 1925, shows the fitting of the belt armor. As mounted on a battle cruiser, the belt was to consist of inclined 254 mm VC armor, but as mounted on an aircraft carrier, the thickness was reduced to 127 mm, as protection against 20.3 cm shells. Because a considerable number of armor plates had already been manufactured, the Steel Division at Kure had to reroll the plates to exactly half the original thickness. It was the first time such work was performed in Japan. Note the position of the armor bolts and the wood backing to the left of the plate that is being positioned. The openings above and to the right are for the 20 cm guns.

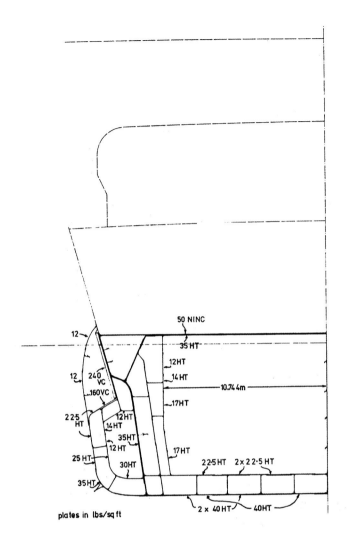

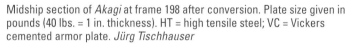

plates in lbs/sq ft

Midship section of *Akagi* at frame 198 after conversion. Plate size given in pounds (40 lbs. = 1 in. thickness). HT = high tensile steel; VC = Vickers cemented armor plate. *Jürg Tischhauser*

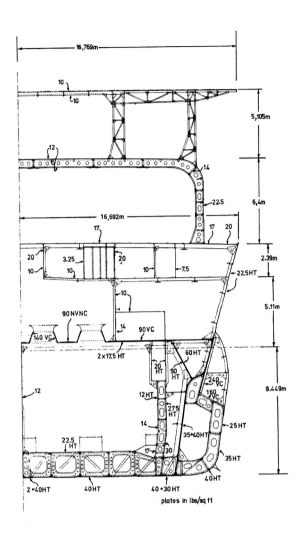

plates in lbs/sq ft

Midship section of *Akagi* at frame 174 after conversion. NVNC = new Vickers noncemented. *Jürg Tischhauser*

CHAPTER 4
Outline Description of Kaga

Flight Decks, Hangars, Elevators, and Avgas Tanks

The main features of the conversion were identical to those of *Akagi*. The three-stage flight deck, the hangars, the aircraft elevators, the armament, and the protection differed only in a few items, the principal reason being the different design origins. *Kaga*, having been designed as a battleship, had a shorter and broader hull. The upper flight deck was therefore only 171.20 m long, despite being extended as far as the stern. In contrast to *Akagi*, it did not slope down toward the stern but ascended. This reversion was chosen because it was desired for the fighters to land over the bow, and this ascent should provide the same effect as *Akagi*'s deck. At around that time there was a rumor that the USN also wanted to apply this method on *Saratoga* and *Lexington*, but in fact, neither the USN nor the IJN applied this method in practice.[1]

Kaga's broader hull allowed the lower flight deck to be wider (24.38 m compared with 22.86 m on *Akagi*). There were also differences in the shapes, particularly at the aft end of the takeoff-and-landing deck, the middle takeoff deck, and the fore part of the lower takeoff deck.

The conversion of *Kaga* was begun later than that of *Akagi*, and the elevators (10.67 m × 15.85 m forward and 12.80 m × 9.15 m aft) were enlarged to take into account the trend toward larger aircraft. Like on *Akagi*, the British longitudinal arrester gear was installed, but it was soon replaced by the Fieux-type transverse cable system, developed by the French Schneider Co. for the aircraft carrier *Béarn*.

Kaga during the imperial special naval review (*tairei tokubetsu kankanshiki*) off Yokohama on December 4, 1928. This photo was taken by Captain (constructor) Makino Shigeru. The massive horizontal funnel arrangement is impressive, but it was a failure and was later rebuilt. It is said that humidity was abnormally high in the compartments adjacent to the long funnels, and also that the hot gases disrupted the airflow, affecting landing operations. *Kure Maritime Museum*

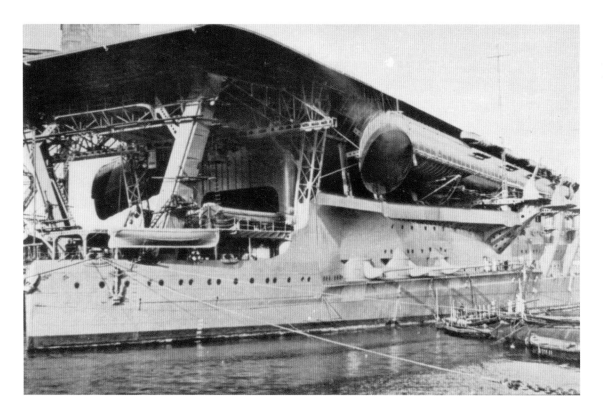

Kaga during fitting-out on December 20, 1928. After the imperial special naval review off Yokohama, *Kaga* returned to Yokosuka Naval Arsenal for further works. The large opening in the middle-deck hangar was used for loading and unloading seaplanes, and the rails and lifting equipment below the upper flight deck can be seen. The protracted construction period was caused by undetermined parts in the planning stage, and construction had to be carried out while the actual ship was still being examined, as well as due to budget restrictions.

Kaga still under fitting-out at Yokosuka Koumi on January 20, 1929. Certain parts of the ship's construction were still undetermined, such as armament and final outfit, and work continued under budget difficulties. The flag at the stern is flying, and on the starboard side aft is a kedge anchor. In the background is the plant of Koumi's machinery department. In the foreground on the left is a shipboard torpedo boat (*suiraitei*). Beyond it are a naval communications boat (*kōtsusen*) and a bridge boat (*hashisen*), using the hull of a former German submarine. Below the 20 cm casemate guns is the arsenal's 20-ton tug (*eisen*) and communications boat (*No. 495*).

Kaga at Yokosuka on December 5, 1929. The form of her stern is markedly different from that of *Akagi*, and from this angle the flight deck appears to be higher at the stern and lower at the forward part. This inclination of the upper flight deck may have been intended (but not actually implemented) for landing of fighters and other aircraft from the bow. Note the white range clock (*renji kurokku*) and the white-painted markings on the flight deck supports for the helm signals.

Kaga during flight training in 1930. During this time the ship embarked type 13 attack planes, type 10 reconnaissance planes, and type 3 fighters. The photo shows a type 13 attack plane landing on the upper flight deck, and the deckhands are rushing to the stopped plane. The flight deck equipment is also visible, with one elevator at the aft part and one at the forward part of the flight deck. The forward elevator has windscreens fitted at the front and rear. The aft elevator was connected to all three hangars, and it was somewhat larger than *Akagi*'s (117.12 m^2 vs. 99.12 m^2). The forward elevator was connected only to the two uppermost hangars, since the lower hangar did not go this far forward. This elevator was also larger than *Akagi*'s (166.24 m^2 vs. 153.40 m^2). Note the marking of the aft end of the flight deck.

Profile and plan of *Kaga* in 1930.
Sekai no Kansen

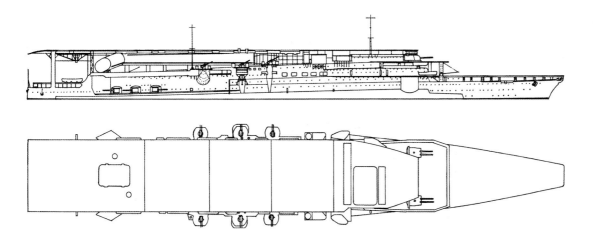

Kaga with aircraft on the flight decks, photographed in 1930. Six type 3 fighters (*kanjō sentōki*) can be seen on the lower flight deck, which was used for takeoffs. Eight type 13 attack planes (*kanjō kōgekiki*) can be seen on the upper flight deck, which was used both for launching and landing planes. When *Kaga* entered service, she embarked forty-eight aircraft plus twelve reserve planes. These comprised twelve type 3 fighters (plus four in reserve), twelve type 0 reconnaissance planes (*kanjō teisatsuki*) (plus four in reserve), and twenty-four type 13 attack planes (plus four in reserve). However, this was the maximum number that could be embarked, and in peacetime operations fewer aircraft were embarked. Note the lowered wireless masts.

Kaga with a small bridge structure in a photo taken in August 1933. This bridge, on the starboard side, had been fitted in May–June 1933 and was called a navigation bridge (*kōkai kankyō*)

Kaga berthed at an unknown location and time. The photo was taken from the port quarter, and smoke is billowing from the port funnel. The structure protruding from the flight deck aft is the aft elevator. This elevator was 12.8 m long and 9.15 m wide, but the elevator was two stage, so that when the top platform (lid) was level with the upper flight deck, the lower platform was at the level of the upper hangar deck. *Kaga's* lower hangar did not extend far enough aft to reach the elevator well, and planes had to be lifted to the middle hangar. In consequence, the lower hangar was almost exclusively used for auxiliary planes. *Maru Special*

Kaga's upper flight deck at the naval review off Yokohama on August 25, 1933. This photo was taken by Captain Furukawa Akira and shows the wooden deck and arrester cables (*chakkan seidō sōchi*). The type of arrester gear was the transverse French Fieux gear, which was vastly superior to the British longitudinal gear. The main purpose of the small island-shaped bridge was for control of the takeoff and landing of planes. Handrails (*tesuri*) can be seen on the flight deck to the left of the bridge, surrounding the forward elevator. There are embedded eyepieces (*mekan* [*aipīsu*]) for aircraft mooring at various places on the wooden deck.

Photo of a hangar aboard *Kaga* during fitting-out, taken on January 20, 1928. Hangar images are quite rare, and this one shows the interior of *Kaga*'s upper hangar, just below the upper flight deck. Work is almost complete, but the wooden supports are still in place. It is said that work inside the hangar was prioritized in preparation for the handover ceremony. The photo is taken in the direction of the bow, and the light may be shining through the open forward elevator. *Sekai no Kansen*

The interior of *Kaga*'s compass bridge about 1928. The steering wheel, the magnetic compass, engine room telegraph transmitters (*right and left*), and voice pipes can be seen. *Kure Maritime Museum*

Kaga's compass bridge on the turret deck in front of the upper hangar on October 20, 1928, about a month after the full-power trials. The deck was originally planned as a takeoff deck for fighters launched directly from the hangar, but this attempt was given up even before completion. The structures at both sides and in front of the bridge are lookout stations (*mihari-sho*). *Kure Maritime Museum*

Propulsion System

Kaga's propulsion system, designed for her configuration as a battleship, remained largely unchanged and consisted of four Kawasaki Brown-Curtis geared-turbine sets developing 91,000 shp on four shafts, for a speed of 26.5 knots. As a result of the reduction in weight from the original normal displacement of 39,900 tons to a 33,639-tonne trial displacement, *Kaga* achieved 27.5 knots on September 15, 1928, and was therefore 5 knots slower than *Akagi*.

As on *Akagi*, steam was supplied by Kampon type B (*Ro*) boilers with a working pressure of 20 kg/cm². However, while *Akagi* had nineteen boilers, *Kaga* had only twelve (eight oil burners and four mixed-fuel burners). All boilers worked with saturated steam. The 3,600 tons of heavy oil and 1,700 tons of coal, a total of 5,300 tons of fuel, gave her the same range as *Akagi*.

A major feature differentiating the two aircraft carriers was the funnel arrangement. On both sides, a broad tube was routed below the takeoff-and-landing deck almost as far as the stern, where the mouth was directed obliquely downward and outward. This method was chosen by the designers because the wind tunnel experiments had not produced an efficient solution, and hence the ships were to be compared for efficiency of exhaust gas elimination. The arrangement was hotly disputed right from the beginning, and several designers, such as Vice Admiral (shipbuilding) Hiraga Yuzuru, who had been responsible for the design of the cruisers from the *Yūbari* to the Myōkō class (as well as many other ships), made very derogatory remarks about it. They were proved absolutely right, since the aim of keeping the hot exhaust gases remote from the flight deck was not achieved, and as a result of *Kaga*'s lower speed, the airflow at the stern was disturbed and landing operations were obstructed. In addition, accommodations for the noncommissioned officers and deck officers, which were located beside the funnels along the ship's sides, was almost uninhabitable. A further disadvantage, if somewhat less important, was the greater weight of more than 100 tons compared with *Akagi*. Altogether *Kaga*'s arrangement was a total failure.

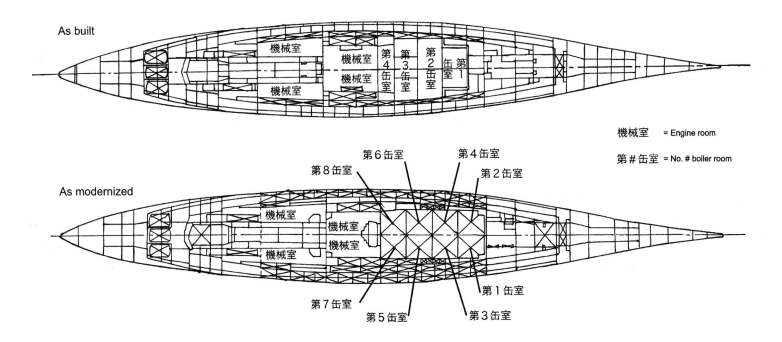

As built

機械室 = Engine room

第 # 缶室 = No. # boiler room

第8缶室　第6缶室　第4缶室　第2缶室

As modernized

第7缶室　第5缶室　第3缶室　第1缶室

Plan of the first hold deck of *Kaga. Sekai no Kansen*

Photo of one of *Kaga*'s original turbines. *Courtesy of Takagi Hiroshi*

Kaga during full-power trials between the pylons off Tateyama on September 15, 1928. In this photo the smoke is cooled by the seawater-cooling system. Her displacement was 33,622 tons, and she reached a speed of 27.6 knots. It has been said that it was decided to fit the very long horizontal funnels in order to compare the arrangement with *Akagi*'s curved funnel. Vice Admiral (constructor) Hiraga Yuzuru regarded *Kaga*'s funnel arrangement as being "absurd." It has also been suggested that the funnel arrangement was fitted because the upper weight of the ship had been reduced when she was converted, and that the funnel arrangement should adjust the roll period.

Armament and Protection

The armament (including fire control) was the same as that on *Akagi*, and the principal revisions for armor protection have been mentioned earlier. Further data will be provided in descriptions of their modernization conversion.

This photo of *Kaga* taken at Yokosuka Koumi on November 20, 1928, shows her during fitting-out. The hull is completely painted and the 20 cm guns in casemates are in place, as are the twin 12 cm high-angle guns on the sponsons. Note the large opening at the aft end of the middle hangar, and the 200-ton crane on the pier. The ship in the background is the old armored cruiser *Iwate*.

The port forward section of *Kaga* at Yokosuka Naval Arsenal on December 20, 1928. The installation of the twin 12 cm high-angle guns appears to be finished. Forward and just below the turret deck (middle flight deck) is the platform for the reserve command station (*yobi shikisho*). The high-angle-gun command station (*kōkakuhō shikisho*) is located forward, just below the upper flight deck. The sloping part, in the vicinity of the scupper pipe, of the hull plating can be seen, and here the armor was 127 mm thick. The lines of the ship appear to be very complex, and this was because the IJN made good use of the hull as already built.

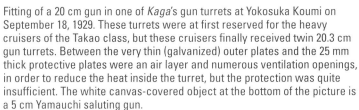

Fitting of a 20 cm gun in one of *Kaga*'s gun turrets at Yokosuka Koumi on September 18, 1929. These turrets were at first reserved for the heavy cruisers of the Takao class, but these cruisers finally received twin 20.3 cm gun turrets. Between the very thin (galvanized) outer plates and the 25 mm thick protective plates were an air layer and numerous ventilation openings, in order to reduce the heat inside the turret, but the protection was quite insufficient. The white canvas-covered object at the bottom of the picture is a 5 cm Yamauchi saluting gun.

One of *Kaga*'s twin 12 cm high-angle guns during battle training in January–March 1932. *Kaga* had six such guns mounted on sponsons, and it is said that the future position of the target was calculated by the antiaircraft director (*kōsha hōiban*). However, due to the low positions of the guns, they could not fire across the upper flight deck. *Sekai no Kansen*

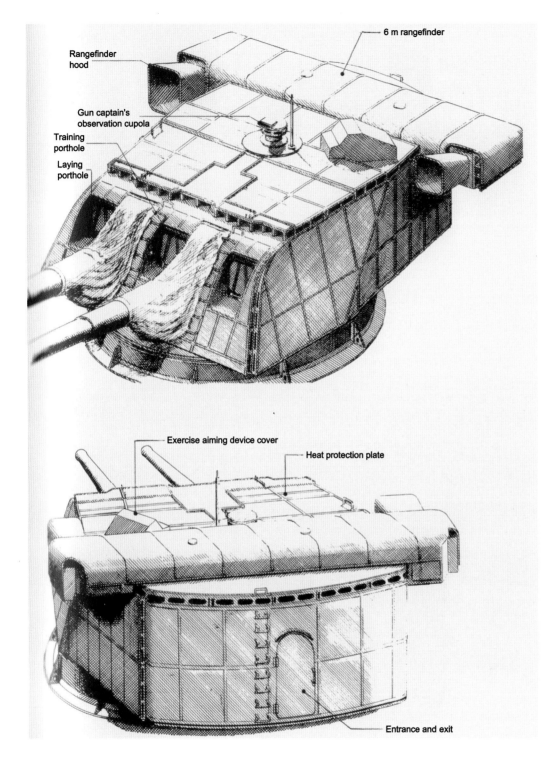

6 m rangefinder

Rangefinder
hood

Gun captain's
observation cupola

Training
porthole

Laying
porthole

Exercise aiming device cover

Heat protection plate

Entrance and exit

Drawing of the exterior of the 50 cal. three-year type no. 2 20 cm in model B turret, mounted on *Akagi* and *Kaga* prior to reconstruction. They were designed by engineer Hata Chiyokichi, but according to historian Tsutsumi Akio (in *Sekai no Kansen* 944), the selection of exactly 20 cm (7.9″) must be considered a serious mistake. Instead, the IJN should have selected 20.32 cm (8″) from the beginning. *Hasegawa Tōichi*

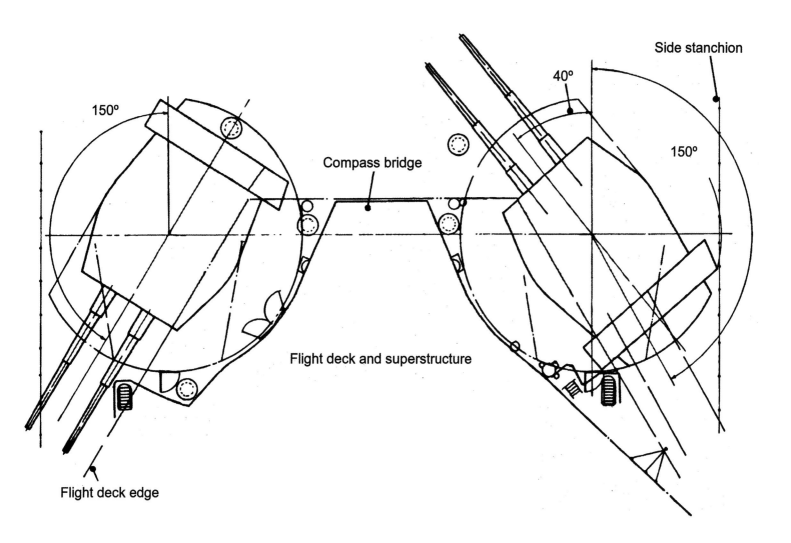

Side stanchion

150°

40°

150°

Compass bridge

Flight deck and superstructure

Flight deck edge

Outline of the 20 cm twin gun turrets aboard *Akagi. Hasegawa Tōichi & Tsutsumi Akio*

Kaga during fitting-out on September 20, 1927, at Yokosuka Koumi. High-angle gun no. 4 (port side) is being fitted, and the waterline armor is being installed. Since most of the ship's armor had already been manufactured, it was rerolled to a thickness of 127 mm.

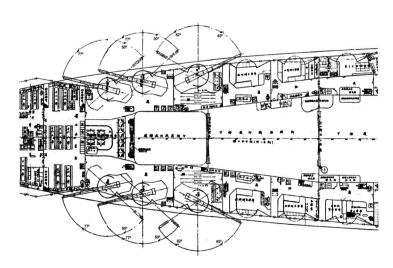

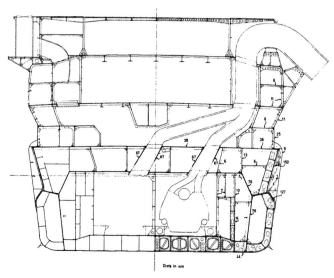

Structural drawing of the 20 cm single casemate guns of *Akagi* (after refit). In wartime it was possible to increase the number of casemate guns by adding six 12 cm guns forward of the existing 20 cm guns. This was, however, never carried out. The starboard 20 cm guns were numbered 1, 3, and 5, the port guns 2, 4, and 6.

Midship section of *Kaga* after conversion. Plate thickness in mm. *Jürg Tischhauser*

CHAPTER 5
Defects Affecting Their Operational Value

When the completed aircraft carriers were assigned to the fleet and used operationally, it was confirmed that the three-stage flight deck did not meet expectations and was unfit for the technically advanced planes, and the small aircraft capacity in relation to the size remarkably limited their fighting power. Their use in the fleet made it obvious how the ships were to be improved. The following improvements were uniformly required:

- one takeoff-and-landing deck, stretched over the whole length
- increase in aircraft capacity
- renewal of the equipment for flight operations
- fitting of an island bridge

Besides these items referring to the particular character of the aircraft carrier, improvement of armament and an increase in machinery performance were requested. In other words, the almost total modernization of the ships was recognized as being necessary.

Prior to the modernization conversion, some revisions were incorporated, such as the fitting of transverse arrester gear, improvement of the radio equipment, improvement of the ventilation system, and the fitting of a small navigation bridge on the takeoff-and-landing deck.

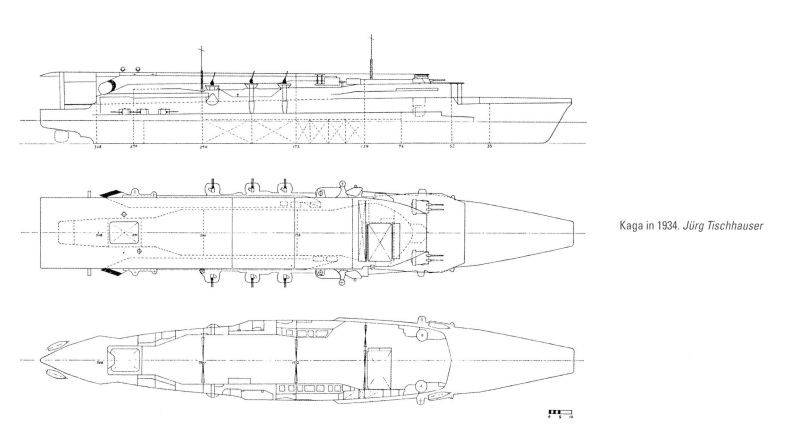

Kaga in 1934. *Jürg Tischhauser*

Principal Particulars of Akagi and Kaga

	Akagi as built	Akagi as modernized	Kaga as built	Kaga as modernized
Builder	Kure Navy Yard	Sasebo Navy Yard	Kawasaki (Kōbe)	Sasebo Navy Yard
Laid down	December 6, 1920	–	July 19, 1920	–
Launched	April 22, 1925	–	November 17, 1921	–
Conversion begun	November 19, 1923	October 24, 1935	November 19, 1923	June 25, 1934
Commissioned	March 25, 1927	August 31, 1938	March 31, 1928	June 25, 1935
Standard displacement (tons)	26,900	36,500	26,900	38,200
Trial displacement (tons)	34,364	41,300	33,693	42,541
Length, oa (m)	261.21	260.67	238.5	247.65
Length, wl (m)	248.95	250.36	230	240.3
Length, pp (m)	234.7	234.7	217.93	217.93
Beam, max. (m)	31	–	31.67	–
Beam, wl (m)	28.96	31.32	29.57	32.5
Draught (m)	8.08	8.71	7.92	9.48
Hull depth to flight deck (m)	29	28.65	29.57	29.57
Freeboard at trial displacement (m)	–	19.46	–	19.7
Length of main flight deck (m)	190.2	249.17	171.3	248.58
Width of flight deck amidships (m)	30.48	30.48	30.48	30.48
Width of flight deck forward (m)	–	19.00	–	14.32
Width of flight deck aft (m)	–	23.77	–	30.48
Number of hangars	3	3	3	3
Number of elevators	2	3	2	3
Size of forward elevator (m)	11.8 × 13	11.8 × 16	10.67 × 15.85	11.5 × 12
Size of midships elevator (m)	–	11.8 × 13	–	10.67 × 15.85
Size of after elevator (m)	12.8 × 8.4	12.8 × 8.4	12.8 × 9.15	12.8 × 9.15
Aircraft capacity:				
Fighters	16 Type 3	12 (+4) Type 96	16 Type 3	12 (+3) Type 96
Torpedo bombers	28 Type 13	38 (+16) Type 96	28 Type 13	36 (+9) Type 95
Dive bombers	–	19 (+5) Type 96	–	24 (+6) Type 94
Reconnaissance	16 Type 10	–	16 Type 10	–
Armament:				
20 cm Type 3	10 (2 × 2, 6 × 1)	6 (6 × 1)	10 (2 × 2, 6 × 1)	10 (10 × 1)
12 cm AA Type 10	12 (6 × 2)	12 (6 × 2)	12 (6 × 2)	–
12.7 cm AA Type 89	–	–	–	16 (8 × 2)
25 mm MG Type 96	–	28 (14 × 2)	–	22 (11 × 2)
Turbines	Gihon	Gihon	Brown Curtis	Kampon
Boilers	19 Kampon Type B	19 Kampon Type B	12 Kampon Type B	8 Kampon Type B
Shp	131,000	133,000	91,000	127,400
Speed (knots)	32.5	31.5	27.5	28.34
Fuel (tons)	3,900 (oil), 2,100 (coal)	5,770 (oil)	3,600 (oil), 1,700 (coal)	7,500 (oil)
Endurance (nm/knots)	8,000/14	8,200/16	8,000/14	10,000/15

Note:
oa = over all; wl = waterline; pp = perpendiculars; AA = anti-aircraft; MG = machine gun; nm = nautical mile

CHAPTER 6
Modernization of Kaga

Although completed later than *Akagi, Kaga* was the first to be modernized, because in her case the hot exhaust gases disturbed the landing of planes and heated up the accommodations to intolerable temperatures. Also, her speed was lower and the flight deck smaller. All in all, her operational value was inferior to *Akagi*'s, and she was therefore more in need of improvement.

Sasebo Naval Arsenal began the modernization conversion on June 25, 1934, and completed it exactly one year later. Her conversion had been approved in May 1933, but financial restrictions had caused several postponements. The principal items included the following:

The former takeoff-and-landing deck was lengthened to 248.58 m, to project slightly over both the bow and the stern, and the two lower takeoff decks were used for extending the two hangars forward. A third elevator was fitted to serve the new hangars. The hangar for the reserve parts was also reconstructed to accommodate more planes. The increased hangar area provided for a maximum stowage of ninety aircraft (12+ [3] type 96 fighters, 36 + [9] type 95 torpedo bombers, 24 + [6] type 94 dive bombers = 72 + [18] planes).[1] The upper platform of the aft elevator was removed to reduce top weight.[2]

She was the first Japanese aircraft carrier fitted with the type 1 crash barrier, developed by the Navy Air Technical Department (*Kaigun Kōkū Gijutsusho*), and the Kure type 4 arrester gear. The type 1 crash barrier was later replaced by a type 3, which was also fitted on *Akagi* during her modernization.

The bomb and torpedo hoists were modified so that they could transport their load directly to the hangars or the flight deck, whereas previously the ordnance had to be transshipped once during the transit. The advantage was a quicker transport; the disadvantage was a remarkably increased danger in case of fire.

Since the former compass bridge had to make way for the extension of the hangars, an island bridge was erected on the starboard side of the flight deck. This provided improved direction for flight operations as well as a better conning position.[3]

To improve the ship's speed, she was fitted with two new Kampon geared-turbine sets in the forward engine rooms, while the original Brown-Curtis geared-turbine sets in the aft engine rooms remained unchanged. The new Kampon turbine sets consisted of one high-pressure, one medium-pressure, one low-

pressure, and one cruising turbine geared to a single shaft. The propellers were replaced by new ones adapted to the new machinery, and the hull was lengthened at the stern by 9.14 m in order to lower hull resistance. The steam for operating the engines was generated by eight type B Kampon oil-fired boilers, with a working pressure of 22 kg/cm^2 at a steam temperature of 300°C. The boilers were of the same type as those fitted in the light/heavy cruisers of the Mogami class, and the two new turbine sets were also identical to those of these cruisers. The boiler rooms were extended forward and subdivided to allow one room per boiler. The arrangement of four turbine sets in four engine rooms and eight boilers in eight boiler rooms was referred to as "ideal" by the IJN. The designed speed was 28.5 knots with 125,000 shp, and on trials *Kaga* achieved 28.34 knots with 127,400 shp at a displacement of 42,700 tonnes. The fuel stowage was modified to 7,500 tons of oil, providing an increased endurance of 10,000 nm at 16 knots.

The former funnels were removed and replaced by the bent type, as applied on *Akagi* before conversion to the oil-fired boilers. Four boilers were bundled into one uptake, and the two uptakes were led in a single casing, and, as on *Akagi*, this was provided with a cooling system and a blind cover. The weight of the funnel was reduced by several hundred tons.

The space on either side of the upper hangar, originally occupied by the funnel ducting, was divided into two decks in order to provide living quarters for the additional air and maintenance crews of the larger aircraft complement.

The antiaircraft armament was improved by replacing the twelve 12 cm high-angle guns with sixteen type 89 40 cal., 12.7 cm high-angle guns in eight twin mountings (starboard: two forward, two aft; port: one forward, three aft), which were fitted in raised sponsons to obtain better firing arcs across the flight deck. For close-range defense, twenty-two type 96 25 mm machine guns in eleven twin mounts were also located in sponsons. There were also six type 11 6.5 mm machine guns.

The complete restructuring of the flight deck necessitated the removal of the twin 20 cm turrets, and these were replaced by two 20 cm guns in casemates on each side, forward of the casemate guns already fitted to maintain the original ten guns. This cannot but be criticized as a great error, and the budget should have been either saved or spent for improvements.

The torpedo bulges were heightened till the middle deck to improve the metacentric height (GM). This caused an increase of the beam and brought about an improvement of stability and lowering of the center of gravity automatically. Some influence was also exerted by the report of the investigation committee of the "*Tomozuru* incident."[4]

The conversion of *Kaga* into an island-type aircraft carrier was not without problems, and both designers and constructors had to solve a large number of serious problems—more than was known at that time[5]—but it was finally a success, and *Kaga* returned to the fleet as the IJN's largest and most powerful aircraft carrier.[6]

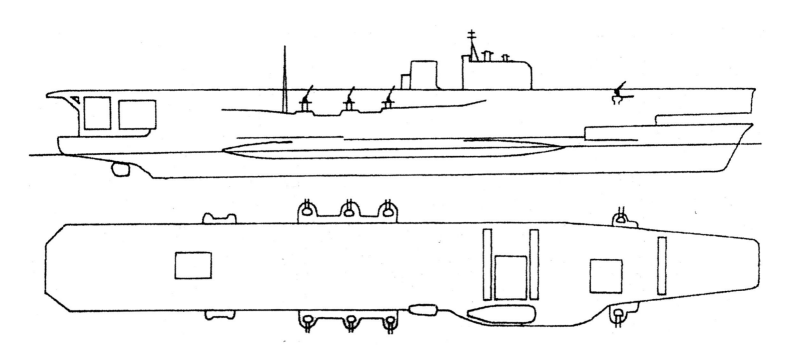

Conversion plan of *Kaga* before March 1934. (1) Flight deck with overhang at the stern, (2) three aircraft elevators, (3) large bridge structure with small tripod signal mast, (4) vertical funnel separated from the bridge structure, and (5) no machine guns visible forward and aft, and only one sponson per side aft of the high-angle gun sponsons. *Waldemar Trojca*

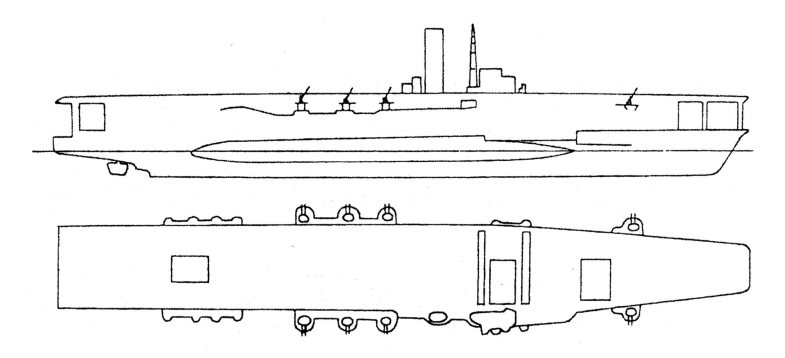

Conversion plan of *Kaga* after March 1934. Plans changed after the *Tomozuru* incident. (1) Enlarged bulges, (2) reduced bridge structure, (3) reduced flight deck length, (4) reduced hangar area, (5) changes in elevators and antiaircraft armament (*not shown*), and (6) thin and high funnel. *Waldemar Trojca*

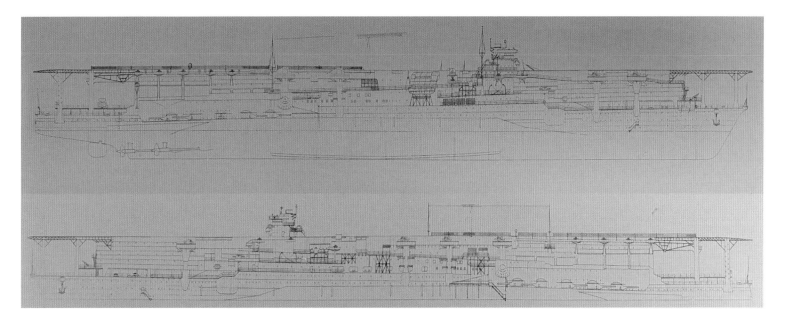

Profile of *Kaga*. *Jürg Tischhauser*

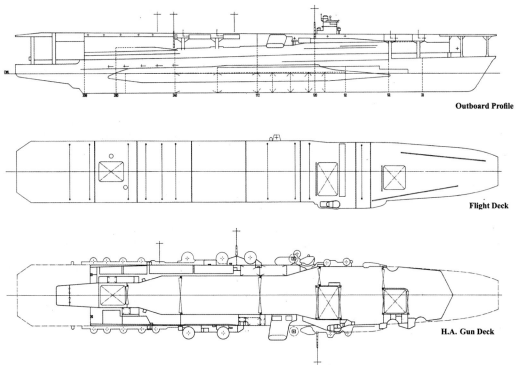

Kaga after conversion. *Jürg Tischhauser*

Outboard Profile

Flight Deck

H.A. Gun Deck

Bridge structure of *Kaga. Wilhelm Besch*

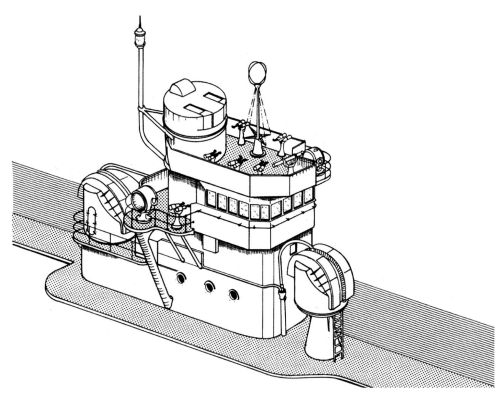

Bridge structure of *Kaga. Hasegawa Tōichi*

Key to top drawing:
1 = 4.5 m high-angle rangefinder, 2 = main gun command station, 3 = targeting device, 4 = type 91 high-angle-gunfire control system, 5 = direction finder

Key to lower drawings:
1 = high-angle-gunfire control system, 2 = 60 cm signal light, 3 = ladder, 4 = flight deck, 5 = 16 m to centerline of flight deck, 6 = upper deck level, 7 = rangefinder deck level, 8 = 12 cm binoculars for air defense control station, 9 = 12 cm binoculars, 10 = 18 cm binoculars for air defense control station, 11 = 1.5 m rangefinder, 12 = 30 cm signal lamp, 13 = repeater compass, 14 = binoculars for air defense control officer, 15 = goniometer (D/F) room, 16 = 2 kW signal lamp, 17 = distribution station for electricity, 18 = repeater compass for type 83 magnetic compass, 19 = 18 cm binoculars, 20 = information station, 21 = steering station, 22 = searchlight control and high-angle lookout direction panel, 23 = takeoff-and-landing control station

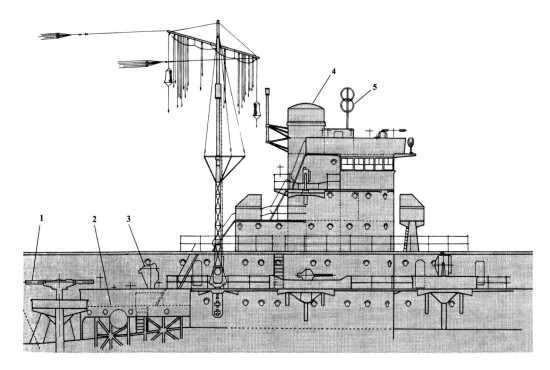

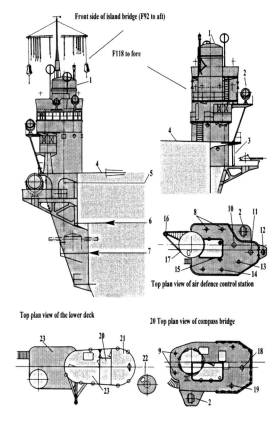

Front side of island bridge (F92 to aft)

F118 to fore

Top plan view of air defence control station

Top plan view of the lower deck

20 Top plan view of compass bridge

Kaga in a photo probably taken in December 1935 at Sasebo, shortly after the conversion at Sasebo Naval Arsenal that lasted from June 25, 1934, to June 25, 1935. As a result of the conversion, the flight deck, which had been divided into three levels, now extended over the full length of the ship, and effectively the size of the flight deck was increased by 45 percent. Together with *Akagi*, *Kaga* constituted the main force of the carrier force. *Kure Maritime Museum*

Kaga as flagship of the 2nd Carrier Division in an official photo taken in 1936. From this perspective, the island bridge is barely visible. The height from the draft line to the flight deck was 19.7 m, which was slightly more than *Akagi*'s (19.46 m). During the reconstruction, her propellers were replaced by new ones of 4.5 m diameter (instead of 4.419 m). Note the machine gun sponsons along the aft part of the flight deck.

Starboard view of *Kaga* after the modernization conversion, taken in 1936. In spite of being converted into an aircraft carrier later than *Akagi*, *Kaga* was modernized earlier because of her lesser capabilities as an aircraft carrier. The flight deck was lengthened to the bow, an island bridge was erected, the propulsion system was greatly improved, the horizontal funnels were removed and replaced by a characteristic Japanese-style bent funnel, and the antiaircraft defense was increased. The appearance of the ship changed completely. The smoke-cooling system is in operation.

View from *Kaga*'s bridge structure looking aft on the starboard side. This photo was taken in May 11, 1937, in Bungo Suido and shows arrester cables on the flight deck, a twin 25 mm machine gun mount, a rangefinder tower with a 4.5 m stereo rangefinder for the high-angle guns, the downward facing funnel, twin 12.7 cm high-angle gun mounts with soot covers and a wireless mast in almost vertical position. Note the personnel in the pockets along the flight deck.

Kaga's rebuilt bridge structure. It was used for navigating the ship, to command air operations, and to control flight deck operations. However, it was very small, and from *Hiryū* onward a new, somewhat large type was used. Note that the collapsed signal mast, with its signal yard, is not level with the flight deck. On top of the bridge structure is a short mast with signal light on top. In front of it is the type 91 high-angle fire control system. A D/F loop antenna is fitted on the middle of the air defense control station (*bōkū shikisho*). Below the compass bridge (with windows) is the lower bridge (*kabu kankyō*). A 60 cm signal light is placed on the aft end of the bridge structure, and below it the searchlight controller and takeoff-and-landing control station. On the level of the flight deck, aircrews could enter the waiting room. *Maru*

Kaga in a photo taken around 1940. Note the conspicuous portside bulge. No aircraft are on the flight deck, and the layout and antiaircraft armament can be seen clearly. From forward can be seen the forward elevator (*zenbu shōkōki*), windshields (*shafūsaku*), the bridge structure with signal mast, the center elevator (*chūbu shōkōki*), the funnel (*entotsu*), the aft elevator (*kōbu shōkōki*), and the red-and-white deck-landing marks (*chakkan hyōshiki*) at the aft end of the flight deck. *Maru Special*

Kaga underway in 1940–41 at an unknown location. This is an exceptionally good view of the flight deck. When reconstructed, the upper flight deck was extended from 171.3 m to 248.58 m, and the light areas in the photo represent the extended areas. The white dotted line is the center of the flight deck. *Kaga* was scheduled to be equipped with a ship launch accelerator (catapult) at the forward end of the flight deck, and preliminary work was carried out and tests were conducted, but it is regrettable that this was never put to practical use. *Kure Maritime Museum*

CHAPTER 7
Modernization of Akagi

After *Kaga*, *Akagi* was also modernized at Sasebo Naval Arsenal from October 24, 1935, to August 31, 1938. Despite a conversion period virtually three times as long as that for *Kaga*, the conversion was far less extensive, the principal reason being financing. Her conversion was oriented in principle on that of *Kaga*, but since they were different ship types, originally, there were naturally differences. The main items were as follows.

As in *Kaga*, the three-stage flight deck was replaced by an extended flight deck of 249.17 m length, although in this case the slope toward the stern was retained. Until *Taihō* was commissioned, *Akagi* (which had meanwhile been sunk) possessed the largest flight deck of the Japanese aircraft carriers (the conversion of the Yamato-class battleship *Shinano* into an aircraft carrier relegated her to third place). The aircraft hangars were enlarged, the sides of the open upper hangar were closed by thin plates, and a third elevator was installed forward. Ammunition transport and refueling systems were improved. In contrast to *Kaga*, the lower hangar, hitherto used for reserve planes and reserve parts, was reconstructed into a storeroom. Despite this "loss," she could carry ninety-one aircraft due to the longer length of the two (upper) hangars (12 + [4] type 96 fighters, 19 + [5] type 96 dive-bombers, plus 35 + [16] type 96 torpedo bombers = 66 operational and 25 reserve planes). She had one more plane than *Kaga*, although that ship could carry older aircraft types.

The most-modern types of arrester gear and crash barrier and also two windscreens were fitted.

Equipment for navigation and control of flight operations was assembled in an island bridge but differed from that of *Kaga* in being fitted to port and located approximately halfway along the ship's length. This was quite a unique position, with no other navy applying it, and the reason will be stated later.

Due to the decision that the ammunition (bombs, torpedoes, shells, bullets) and avgas storages had to permit three attacks of all aircraft, besides carrying out extensive reconnaissance flights, the ammunition magazines below the armor deck and the avgas tanks, situated mainly forward outside the armored vital area, were enlarged.

The original turbines were retained, and the only modifications to the machinery were the replacement of the mixed burning boilers by oil-fired units and the improvement of the ventilation performance. However, the general arrangement—that is, to arrange the ventilation ducts on one side only and the exhaust ducts at the opposite side—was maintained and proved to be an error of great consequence in carrier battles, particularly at Midway.

Due to the weight increase during the modernization, *Akagi*'s speed dropped slightly, and on the official trial run she attained only 31.2 knots with 133,000 shp at a displacement of 41,200 tonnes.

Her new heavy oil fuel storage of 5,770 tons provided an endurance of 8,200 nautical miles (nm) at 16 knots.

The shape of the small funnel, which had previously been used for the oil-fired boilers and was angled upward behind the cranked funnel, was matched to that of the large one and enclosed in the same casing, giving *Akagi* a truly mammoth funnel. A smokescreen system (black smoke) was also fitted.

As on *Kaga*, the extension of the flight deck and the upper hangar necessitated the removal of the two 20 cm gun turrets, but in this case—and fortunately—no additional casemate guns were fitted due to the lack of finances. Financing was also the reason that the original type 10 45 cal., 12 cm, high-angle guns, carried in type G mountings low down in ineffective positions, were not replaced by the modern type 89 12.7 cm, high-angle guns, and the height of the sponsons was not changed as on *Kaga*. However, twenty-eight type 96 25 mm machine guns were fitted for close-range antiaircraft defense in fourteen twin mountings (three forward and four aft in sponsons on each side).

Aircraft Equipment		
	Akagi (1938)	**Kaga (1935)**
Hangars	3	3
Aircraft	18 fighters, 18 dive bombers, 27 attack planes	18 fighters, 18 dive bombers, 27 attack planes
Size of flight deck	249.174 × 30.480 m	248.576 × 30.480 m
Aircraft elevators	3	3
Arrester gear	Kure Type Model 4; 10 engines; 10 cables	Kure Type Model 4; 8 engines; 8 cables
Crash barriers	Kūshō Type Model 3 × 5 (2 fixed, 3 portable)	Kūshō Type Model 3 × 4 (2 fixed, 2 portable)
Wind breaks	2	1
Bomb hoists	Lift type × 2	Lift type × 2

Comparison between the Type 10-Year 12 cm High-Angle Gun and the Type 89 12.7 cm High-Angle Gun		
Gun type	**45 cal. 10 year type 12 cm HAG**	**40 cal. 89 type 12.7 cm HAG**
Bore (mm)	120	127
Barrel length oa (m)	5.604	5.284
Bore length oa (m)	5.400	5.080
Bore length (cal.)	45	40
Barrel weight (t)	left gun 2.962, right gun 2.924	3.058
Max. bore pressure (normal service charge) (kg/mm^2)	26.4–26.5	25.0–25.3
Rifling	uniform right	uniform right
Number of grooves	34	36
Total weight of twin mount (t)	22.3	29
Elevation (°)	-10 to +75	-8 to +90
Elevation speed (°/s)	6.5 (manual)	12 (electric motor)
Training speed (°/s)	10 (manual)	6–7 (electric motor)
Ammunition type	Fixed	fixed
Projectile weight (kg)	20.4	23
Projectile length (mm)	414.5	436.5
Propellant weight (kg)	5.2	4.0
Total ammunition weight (kg)	33.5	34.6
Total ammunition length (mm)	1,068	971
Muzzle velocity (m/s)	825	720
Maximum range (m)	15,600	14,600
Maximum altitude (m)	10,400	9,700
Maximum firing rate (rounds/min)	11	14

Sources:
Hans Lengerer & Tomoko Rehm-Takahara, *Warship 1991*, pp. 99–100; Tsutsumi Akio, *Sekai no Kansen* 944: 116.

Trials data							
Ship / state		Trial displacement (tonnes)	Speed (knots)	Power (shp)	Propeller speed (rpm)	Carried out	
						Location	Date
Akagi	as built	34,500	32.59	136,872	215.3	Sata-misaki	1926-11-10
	as rebuilt	41,393	30.18	126,553	207	–	–
Kaga	as built	33,622	27.6	96,851	214.4	Uraga Suidō	1928-09-15
	as rebuilt	43,406	28.58	130,342	forward engines 272 after engines 209	Koshikijima	1935-10-24

Source:
Abe Yasuo, _Sekai no Kansen_, no. 944, p. 107.

Notes:
Tonnes = metric tons (1,000 kg); shp = shaft horsepower; rpm = revolutions per minute.

Profile and plan of _Akagi_. Michael Wünschmann

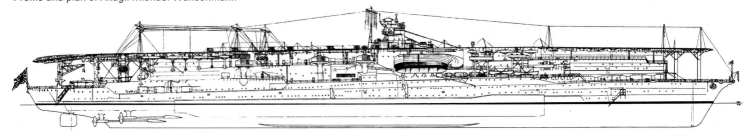

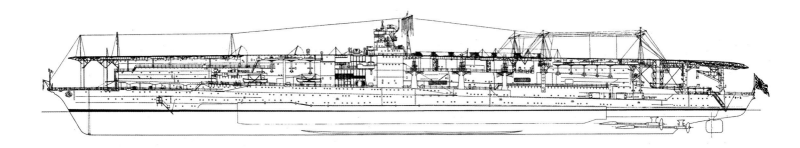

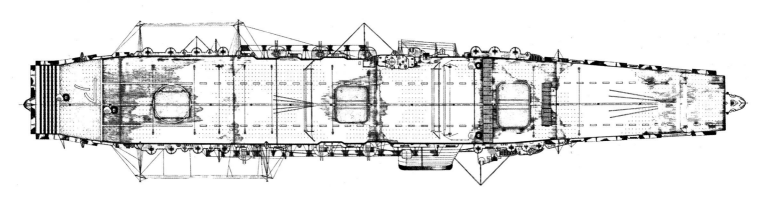

Akagi after conversion. *Jürg Tischhauser*

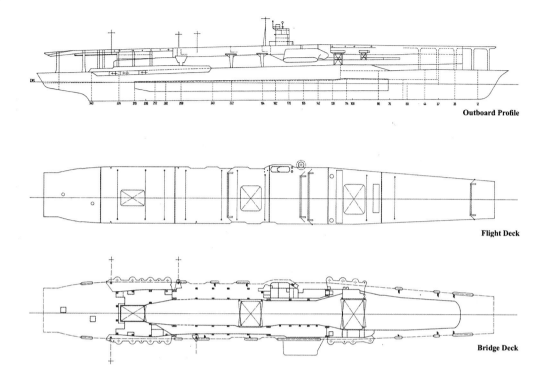

Outboard Profile

Flight Deck

Bridge Deck

Perspective view of *Akagi. Jürg Tischhauser*

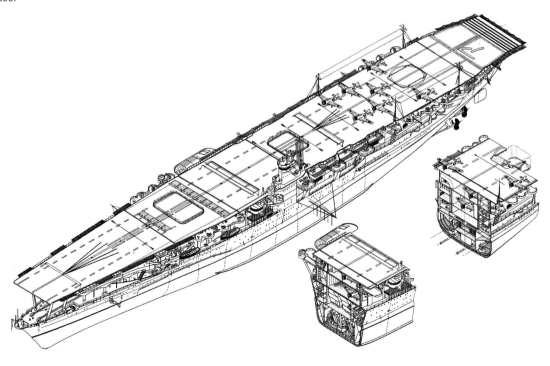

Bridge structure and signal mast of *Akagi*. During reconstruction, both *Akagi* and *Kaga* were fitted with three type 91 high-angle gunfire control systems (port, starboard, and atop the island). *Wilhelm Besch*

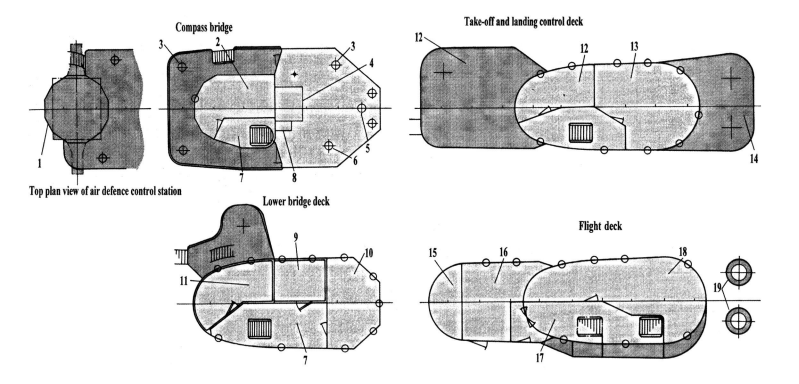

Compass bridge

Take-off and landing control deck

Top plan view of air defence control station

Lower bridge deck

Flight deck

Bridge structure of *Akagi. Hasegawa Tōichi*

Key:
1 = distribution station for electricity, 2 = information station, 3 = 12 cm binoculars, 4 = sea chart box, 5 = type 93 magnetic compass, 6 = 15 cm binoculars, 7 = passageway, 8 = war diary table, 9 = goniometer (D/F) room, 10 = steering station, 11 = no. 3 wireless telephone room, 12 = aft takeoff-and-landing control room, 13 = sea chart and operation room, 14 = forward takeoff-and-landing control room, 15 = storeroom for signal flags, 16 = meteorological operation room, 17 = passageway, 18 = waiting room for pilots, 19 = support tube

Akagi off Yokosuka in late 1938 to January 1939, in a photo taken by the navy ministry. *Akagi* was rebuilt at Sasebo Naval Arsenal after the reconstruction of *Kaga*, and it was completed in August 1938. After this, *Akagi* immediately returned to her home port, Yokosuka, where additional work was carried out. As of December 15, she was incorporated into the fleet and formed the 1st Carrier Division with the accompanying destroyers. This photograph was lent by the navy ministry's popularization bureau (*Fukyūbu*) to the model builder Kawamoto Hachirō for the purpose of producing a model to be presented to His Imperial Highness the Crown Prince. On July 21, 1939, His Majesty the Emperor visited the Combined Fleet and observed the training of the fleet at the entrance of Tokyo Bay. Judging from the machine-gun post structures on both sides of the rear of the flight deck, it is clear that the photograph was taken before August 1939. It was probably taken between December 1938 and January 1939, when *Akagi* sailed to the Combined Fleet's assembly point.

Another photo of *Akagi* taken between December 1938 and January 1939, when she was assigned to the 1st Fleet's 1st Carrier Division. The main items of the refit included a single flight deck; enlarged hangars and an increased number of aircraft carried; an increase in the bomb, torpedo, and aviation fuel load (equivalent to three sorties), with enhanced antiaircraft armament and related equipment; improved engines and funnels; extended cruising range; and enlarged bulges. It is often said that the conversion of the eight mixed-fuel boilers was carried out at the time of this major refit, but historical documents dated April 24, 1930, indicate that the conversion to fuel-oil boilers had already been carried out by 1932. The maximum number of aircraft carried on board after conversion was nineteen type 96 dive-bombers (*kanbaku*) (plus five spares), thirty-five type 96 attack planes (*kankō*) (plus sixteen spares), and twelve type 96 fighters (*kansen*) (plus four spares), with the total number of disassembled spare aircraft reaching ninety-one. Note the single downward-facing funnel, which was combined with the upward-facing funnel to make a larger single funnel. A removable lid was fitted at the top, rear, of the funnel, so that in an emergency the smoke could be directed upward. The antiaircraft guns, machine guns, and some of the aircraft on board have been censored, probably because they were loaned to an outsider. Mr. Kawamoto Hachirō was careful about the handling of the two photos loaned to him, but in 1952 they were presented to the historian Fukui Shizuo. On March 28, 1941, His Imperial Highness the Crown Prince of Japan visited the Yokosuka Naval Arsenal, and it is assumed that a model of this ship was presented as a commemorative gift.

The 12 cm high-angle guns on strict antiaircraft alert aboard *Akagi*, photographed on December 7, 1941. This picture was taken on the port side of *Akagi* and shows twin gun mounts no. 4 (*second from the bow on the port side*) and no. 2 (*in the background*). Presumably the photo was taken from no. 6 gun mount. *Akagi* was never equipped with the more modern twin 12.7 cm high-angle guns, so the ship remained with these rather-outdated guns. Note the flag of Vice Admiral Nagumo Chūichi flown on the signal mast, the shrapnel protection ropes (*danpen bōgyoyō rōpu*), and the low position of the 12 cm guns, thus restricting the fire to only the same side (port). The reason for mounting the guns in such an unfavorable position must have been to preserve the ship's stability.

View of one of *Akagi*'s starboard-side 12 cm high-angle guns fitted with a soot shield. Note the folded wireless masts. This photo was taken during the Hawaii operation, and *Akagi* is followed by *Kaga* and *Zuikaku*. *Maru*

Illustration of a covered twin 12 cm mount aboard *Akagi*. The cover was fitted to protect the personnel from smoke and heat from the funnel. *Futabasha*

The aircraft carrier *Akagi* on her way home from the attack on Pearl Harbor. The exact date of this photograph is unknown, but it is assumed from the appearance of the ship that it was taken on the return trip. Three "Zero" fighters can be seen at the forward end of the flight deck. Although *Akagi*'s exterior was completely redesigned, the ship's interior structure was complicated with many dead ends due to repeated modifications, and there were many problems such as deteriorated habitability and outbreaks of infectious diseases due to inadequate ventilation. Some of the living quarters behind the funnel were uninhabitable due to the fear of carbon monoxide poisoning (they were called murder tenements [*hitogoroshi nagaya*]), and some crew members slept in the hangars. During the reconstruction, *Akagi*'s bulges were enlarged and the waterline beam was increased from 28.96 to 31.32 m. This increase partly explained the slight speed drop.

The bridge structure of *Akagi*, photographed on December 6, 1941. Note the mantelets around the "island." In the right foreground is a 4.5 m high-angle rangefinder, used for target ranging of the 12 cm twin antiaircraft guns. To the left of the rangefinder is a loop antenna. On top of the air defense command post (*bōkū shiki-sho*) is another loop antenna, a 1.5 m rangefinder, and a 7.7 mm machine gun. The bridge structure had four levels: the first level contained the crew embarkation and standby room (*tōjōin taiki shitsu*), the second level the operations room and chart room (*sakusen shitsu ken kaizu shitsu*), the third level the steering room (*sōda shitsu*), and the fourth level the compass bridge (*rashin kankyō*).

CHAPTER 8
Evaluation of the Conversions and Identification Marks

Through the modernization conversion, which was more complete on *Kaga* than on *Akagi*, the decisive properties as aircraft carriers were significantly improved, and both returned to the fleet as the most-powerful aircraft carriers, even if some unfavorable items remained in reference to modern air battle: for instance, the 12 cm high-angle guns in their very low positions on *Akagi*, and the fitting of the formerly turreted 20 cm low-angle guns in casemates on *Kaga*. Another great disadvantage was the technical level of the fire control systems for the high-angle and the machine guns.

As identification marks between these two ships after their modification conversion, three clearly visible and characteristic marks can be noted:[1]

Position of the island bridge: on *Akagi*, to port about amidships; on *Kaga*, to starboard at about 0.35 length

Shape and position of the funnel: *Akagi* had a very broad funnel bent downward and projecting out of the hull forward of the island bridge on the starboard side; the funnel of *Kaga* was considerably smaller and also projected on the starboard side but aft of the island bridge.

Visibility of bow and stern from bird's-eye view: *Akagi*'s bow and stern were well visible below the flight deck; on *Kaga*, both were hidden by the flight deck.

Stability of Akagi and Kaga in Aircraft Carrier Configuration						
Ship	**Akagi**			**Kaga**		
Item/condition	trial	full load	light load	trial	full load	light load
Displacement	41,300	43,849	34,891	41,733	44,760	34,664
Draught	9.2	9.69	7.97	9.321	9.912	7.943
KG	9.7	9.38	10.72	10.132	9.760	11.289
GM	2.38	2.37	1.85	2.338	2.650	1.579
OG	0.50	-0.31	2.75	0.811	-0.152	3.346
Range	85	89.2	74.8	77.3	83	65.5
GZ	2.185	2.28	1.805	1.570	1.692	1.094
A/Aw	1.975	1.83	2.35	2.20	2.0	2.86

Source:
Fukuda Keiji, "Outline of the Fundamental Design of Warships," *Gunkan Kihon Keikaku Shiryō*, p. 78.

Notes:
(1) KG = height of center of gravity above base; GM = metacentric height; OG = height of center of gravity above waterline; Range = range of stability; GZ = maximum righting lever; A/Aw = ratio of lateral plan above/below waterline.
(2) For *Akagi* values as of August 1937; for *Kaga* stability planning values.

Ratios & Coefficients of Akagi and Kaga in Configuration as Battle Cruiser/Battleship and Aircraft Carrier

Ship	Akagi		Kaga	
Item/condition	planning as BC	trial cruise CV (conversion)	planning as BB	trial cruise CV (mod. conversion)
Ratios				
Lwl/Bwl (Length-to-beam ratio)	7.97	9.23	7.380	7.8/7.35
Bwl/d (Beam-to-draft ratio)	3.26	3.85	3.35	3.73/3.41
Lwl/D (Length-to-depth ratio)	16.3	14.7		
D/d (Depth-to-draft ratio)	1.62	2.10		
d/Lwl (Draft-to-length ratio)	0.378	0.325	0.45	0.0344/0.0317
Coefficients				
Block coefficient (Cb)	0.552	0.545	0.581	0.578/0.549
Prismatic coefficient (Cp)	0.604	0.564	0.600	0.590/0.577
Amidships section coefficient (Φ)	0.974	0.966	0.969	0.978/0.951
Waterline coefficient (Cwl)	0.659	0.667	0.677	0.681/0.636

Source:
Fukuda Keiji, "Outline of the Fundamental Design of Warships," *Gunkan Kihon Keikaku Shiryō*, pp. 2, 8, 9. For the values as battle cruiser / battleship, those for *Amagi* and *Tosa* were used.

Notes:
(1) The block coefficient is the ratio between the volume of displacement and that of a rectangular block whose edges are equal to the length, beam, and draft, respectively.
(2) The prismatic coefficient is the ratio between the volume of displacement and that of a cylinder with the same length as the ship and a cross section equal to the area of the amidships section (Φ) below the designed waterline (A Φ).
(3) The amidships section coefficient is the ratio between A Φ and a rectangle with sides equal to beam and depth.
(4) The waterline coefficient is the ratio between the area of designed waterline and the circumscribing rectangle.

Kaga after the modernization conversion, viewed from the port side, about 1938. The primary objectives of the conversion were to increase the number of aircraft carried, extend the flight deck as much as possible by reducing the original three-stage to just a single deck, improve the problematic design of the funnels, install bridge structures on the flight deck, increase the ship's range, and upgrade the anti-aircraft armament. A particularly strong desire from the operators was to improve the ship's speed. As a result, the conversion was an extensive and large-scale operation.

Weight Distribution of Akagi and Kaga in the Battle Cruiser / Battleship and Aircraft Carrier Configurations

Ship	Akagi			Kaga		
Item/condition	BC	CV	%	BB	CV	%
Hull	12,187.16	15,997	38.8	11,540	16,230	38.2
Fittings	1,843.44	2,297	5.55	1,597	2,598	6.04
Armor	8,450.9	8,890	21.5	8,622	3,853	9.06
Protection	5,708.7	included in armor		5,733	5,589	13.1
Equipment, permanent	523.8	377.5	0.91	1,101	385	0.91
Equipment, consumable	525.0	786.5	1.9	included in permanent	881	2.08
Armament, guns	5,920.1	959.6	2.32	6,169.6	1,490	3.05
Armament, torpedoes	177,7	148.3	0.36	171.9	146	0.34
Armament, electric	477.0	690.0	1.67	412.35	716	1.68
Armament, nautical						
Armament, aviation		998.3	2.42		758	4.78
Machinery	4,350.0	4,818	11.67	3,620	3,632	8.5
Fuel, heavy oil		3,800	9.3	700 + 300	5,472	12.9
Light oil (gasoline)		325			341	0.8
Lubricating oil		92.5 + 34			34 + 75	0.08
Reserve feed water		242			180	0.42
Margin		325.4			- 16	
Ballast		146.4			200	
Unknown		322.5				
Total	41,188	41,300		39,967	42,542	100

Source:
Fukuda Keiji, "Outline of the Fundamental Design of Warships," *Gunkan Kihon Keikaku Shiryō*, pp. 39, 42, 43.

Notes:
(1) In case of the battle cruiser / battleship configuration, "normal displacement" is stated.
(2) For *Akagi* "full load displacement" after modernization conversion is stated. However, the heavy-oil storage does not fit. In the "trial displacement" (38,201 tonnes), the fuel storage is stated as 3,847 tonnes.
(3) In the column "Lubricating oil," the second value is for aircraft.
(4) The weight of "nautical instruments" must be included in another "armament weight."
(5) In the column "heavy oil," the second value for *Kaga* in the battleship configuration is "coal," but the values are doubtful.
(6) Pay attention to the great increase of hull weight and the reduction of "armor + protection" and the "gun" weights in the aircraft carrier configuration.

Complement		
Item/ships	Akagi	Kaga
Source	Directive 169 of 23 April 1937; amendment 784, 1941	Directive 169 of 23 April 1937; amendment 784, 1941
Officers	77	77
Special service officers	42	42
Warrant officers	58	58
Petty officers	507	509
Seamen	946	1,022
Total	1,630	1,708

CHAPTER 9
Shipbuilding Conception after the Decision to Convert Akagi and Kaga into Aircraft Carriers

The naval general staff finished the preparation of the 1924 Auxiliary Warship Supplement Program (*Taishō 13 Nendō Hōjō Kantei Hojō Keikaku*) early in 1924. With the goal to strengthen the IJN to the minimal requirements for national defense, 115 war vessels were to be built in six years from fiscal year 1925 to fiscal year 1930. Among the ships were also one standard aircraft carrier of 27,000 tons and three "aircraft supply ships" (*kōkūhokyūkan*) of 10,000 tons each.[1] By 1923 the Japanese press had reported that the third standard aircraft carrier would be built only after experiences with *Amagi* and *Akagi* had been gained, but the naval general staff wanted to increase the power to the total permitted tonnage as quickly as possible. The "aircraft supply ships" were to be used as auxiliary aircraft carriers. Their displacement had been so chosen that they were outside the treaty regulations even though they were to carry out the duties of regular aircraft carriers, within the limits of their size.

The final step of the program preparation was the conference between the chief of the naval general staff, Admiral Yamashita Gentarō,[2] and the navy minister, Admiral Murakami Kakuichi,[3] on February 5, 1924. Because Japan's finances did not permit the execution of such a huge program, reductions were unavoidable. However, on June 11, 1924, Katō Takaaki took over the post of prime minister from Kiyoura Keigo, and a new navy minister was also appointed.

When the new minister, Admiral Takarabe Takeshi, submitted the program to the Finance Commission on September 13, 1924, the content was reduced by forty-two ships (four submarines and thirty-eight auxiliary types, the latter including the three "aircraft supply ships"). Despite the reduction to seventy-three warship types, with the aircraft carrier as the largest one, and "some other types," the Finance Commission rejected the program as too expensive, whereupon it was not submitted to the Diet.

In the following year the 1925 Auxiliary Warship Supplement Program was prepared. Within a period of five years from fiscal year 1926 to fiscal year 1930, forty-nine overaged ships were to be scrapped and replaced by forty-three new ones. The drafting of February 24, 1925, contained two "aircraft supply ships"; the large aircraft carrier and one "supply ship" had been canceled. On March 9, a seaplane tender (*suijōkibokan*) was added as a replacement of *Wakamiya*, that would be twenty-five years old in 1926. Before the program was submitted to the Finance Commission, another revision was made, and when submitted on October 26, 1925, only the 8,000-ton seaplane tender was included; the "aircraft supply ships" had "disappeared."

Irrespective of the considerable reductions, this program shared the fate of the 1924 program. The Finance Commission rejected it except for four destroyers, because the government opposed the expansion of the military forces since it meant increased expenses.

After the passing of the budget of four destroyers in the fifty-first Diet session (December 26, 1925–March 26, 1926), Admiral Takarabe submitted a modified draft of the 1925 program to the Finance Commission on August 5, 1926. Thirty-three ships were to be built with continuous expenses from fiscal year 1927 to fiscal year 1930. The seaplane tender was still included and was to be built with expenditures of fiscal year 1929. The Finance Commission reduced the content to eighteen ships in the same month and also canceled the seaplane tender.

Immediately before the opening of the fifty-second Diet session, Emperor Yoshihito died on December 24, 1926, and his son Hirohito succeeded to the throne. The fifteenth year of the Taishō era also became the first year of the Shōwa era.

The navy minister submitted the original version of the program to the Diet,[4] which permitted the budget of ¥261,310,040 as continuous expenses of fiscal year 1927 to fiscal year 1931 for the construction of twenty-seven warships as the 1927 New Warship Building Supplementary Program (*Shōwa 2 Nendō Kantei Shin Hojū Keikaku*). Among them was also the seaplane tender, required since 1925. At that time, fierce arguments were raging about aircraft carrier size. The point of controversy was whether a small ship such as *Hōshō* or big ships such as *Akagi* and *Kaga* would be best able to survive the damage that inevitably would be sustained in air attacks. It was also argued that a big aircraft carrier almost certainly would lose its operability if the flight deck was damaged, and that a larger number of smaller aircraft carriers had obvious advantages. Irrespective of the planning as the replacement of the overaged seaplane tender (but officially rated aircraft carrier) *Wakamiya*, it was eventually decided to build the

seaplane tender as a prototype small aircraft carrier outside the treaty limitations; she later became *Ryūjō*.

The table on the following page shows the difficult process of the 1927 New Warship Building Supplementary Program from the requirement of the naval general staff until the voting of the Diet in the fifty-second session and promulgation on March 29, 1927, after the emperor's sanction.

In retrospect, the shipbuilding policy after the decision to convert *Akagi* and *Kaga* into aircraft carriers shows that the original planning from 1924 until 1927 covered one standard aircraft carrier, three aircraft supply ships, and one seaplane tender. In the end, only the budget for the seaplane tender passed as the replacement ship for *Wakamiya*.

Ryūjō during full-power trials off Tateyama on April 12, 1933. She is steaming at 29.5 knots, and although the sea is calm the bow waves are high, and this caused the forecastle deck to be raised later. Despite the slim cruiser hull the ship with its box like structure looks overweight.

Process until Passing of the 1927 New Warship Building Supplementary Program							
Types/date	Requirement NGS, Feb. 5, 1924	Proposed by NM, Sep. 13, 1924	Replacement of old ships, Feb. 24, 1925	Proposed by NM, Oct. 26, 1925	Proposed by NM, Aug. 5, 1926	Decision of FM, Oct. 9, 1926	Vote of Diet, 52nd session, Mar. 1927
CV, 27,000 ts	1	1	–	–	–	–	–
Scout C, 10,000 ts	12	12	10,000 ts × 4	4 (replacement)	4	2	10,000 ts × 4
DD	36, 1,900 ts class	36	22	20 (replacement)	15, 1,700 ts class	9	1,700 ts × 15
SS, cruiser	8, 2,000 ts class	10	2	1 (replacement)	1, 2,500 ts class	–	2,500 ts × 1
SS, large	14, 1,500 ts class		8	4 (replacement)	4, 1,650 ts class	4	1,630 ts × 3
SS, minelayer	2, 2,500 ts class	–	–	–	–	–	–
SS, supply	4, 2,500 ts class	–	–	–	–	–	–
Minelayer	2, 5,000 ts class	–	4	2 (replacement)	–	–	–
Aircraft supply ship	3, 10,000 ts class	–	2	–	–	–	–
Repair ship	1, 2,000 ts class	–	–	1 (replacement of sunken ship)	1, 10,000 ts class	–	–
Tanker	2, 15,400 ts	–	1, high speed	1 (replacement)	1, 10,000 ts	–	–
Ammunition transport	1, 15,000 ts class	–	–	–	–	–	–
Light minelayer	12, 1,200 ts class	–	–	–	2, 1,200 ts class	–	1,200 ts × 1
Fast netlayer	1, 5,000 ts class	–	–	–	–	–	–
Kijunmōtei	4, 500 ts class	–	–	–	–	–	–
Hokakumōtei	6, 500 ts class	–	–	–	–	–	–
GB, large	1, 1,000 ts class	–	–	1 (replacement)	–	–	–
GB, medium	1, 820 ts class	–	–	–	1, 820 ts class	1	–
GB, small	4, 340 ts class	–	–	2 (replacement)	2, 250 ts class	2	250 ts × 2
Other	–	Some	–	1 (replacement)	1, 8,000 ts AV	–	8,000 ts × 1
Total	115	Approx. 73	43	37	33	18	27
Fiscal year	1925–1930, continuous budget 6 years	1925–1930, continuous budget 6 years	1926–1930, continuous budget 5 years	1926–1930, continuous budget 5 years	1927–1930, continuous budget 4 years	–	1927–1931, continuous budget 5 years
Note		Requirement of NGS attached		Mar. 9, 1925, NGS required additional supplement of 1 aircraft supply ship, 4 GBs, 1 repair ship			Budget problem: AV (suijōkibokan) was built as CV (kōkūbokan), later Ryūjō

Source:
Senshi Sōsho, Kaigun Gunsembi, vol. 31, no. 1: 343–347.

Notes:
(1) The column of the passing of four 1,700-ton-class destroyers (Tokkei/Fubuki class) is omitted.
(2) Among the reasons stated by Navy Minister Takarabe on October 26, 1925, for the reduction to 37 ships, the following one deserves particular attention: "Considering the development of aircraft, the tactics for their operational use have been taken to reduce the number of surface ships."
(3) The oil tanker was the replacement of *Noma*, which originally was a British wartime rapidly built ship; the repair ship was the replacement of *Kantō*, the only ship of this type sunk in 1924; the two CMs were the replacements *Aso* and *Tokiwa*, converted from old armored cruisers.
(4) The seaplane tender was the replacement of *Wakamiya*, exceeding the age of 25 years (completed as CVL *Ryūjō*).
(5) *Kijunmōtei* = standard netlayer; *Hokakumōtei* = indicator netlayer
(6) NGS = navy general staff; NM = navy minister; FM = finance minister; CV = aircraft carrier; CVL = light aircraft carrier; C = cruiser; DD = destroyer; SS = submarine; GB = gunboat; AV = seaplane tender

CHAPTER 10
Operational Histories

Akagi: Prewar Service

Akagi was laid down, as battleship no. 5 of the Eight-Eight Fleet Completion Program of 1920, at Kure Naval Arsenal on December 6, 1920. Construction was interrupted on February 5, 1922, and then resumed on November 9, 1923, after conversion of her design to an aircraft carrier. She was launched on April 22, 1925, and commissioned on March 25, 1927.

On August 1, 1927, *Akagi* took her place in the Combined Fleet and, shortly after, participated in the main fleet maneuvers. As early as November 1, 1927, she was classified as a first reserve ship (first class), and exactly one month later Captain Kobayashi Seizaburō assumed command of the carrier. On April 1, 1928, *Akagi* and *Hōshō* formed the First Carrier Division, which was placed under the command of the Combined Fleet. For the fleet maneuvers, one carrier was allotted to the IJN's own "blue" forces, and one to the "red" enemy fleet, and for the first time in the history of the IJN her fleets fought a mock battle using carrier aircraft. After this, the First Carrier Division was disbanded and *Akagi* returned to her status of first reserve on December 10, 1928, at which time Captain Yamamoto Isoroku (later commander in chief of the Combined Fleet) assumed command. On April 1, 1929, the ship again became part of the First Carrier Division and participated in the spring maneuvers—during which, on April 20, a storm forced aircraft to make emergency landings in the water off Saishū-dō (today Jeju Island). The carrier returned to Sasebo on April 22. Captain Yamamoto was in command of *Akagi* for just under twelve months, and on November 1, 1929, the ship received a new commander in Captain Kitagawa Kiyoshi. On the thirtieth of that month, the carrier was again classified as a first reserve ship and did not return to her place in the First Carrier Division until December 1, 1930, on which date Captain Wada Hideho assumed control. He was replaced by Captain Ōnishi Jirō on August 28, 1931, after being struck and injured by a landing aircraft on August 18. Ōnishi remained in command for only about three months, with Captain Shibayama Masaki taking over the vessel on December 1, 1931.

Classification as a second reserve ship on December 1, 1931, indicated her preparation for refit, and at Yokosuka Naval Arsenal the ventilation equipment and the radio system were overhauled and improved. Exactly one year later, *Akagi* became a first reserve ship again and, starting on April 25, 1933, resumed her active service by joining the Second Carrier Division and taking part in the special fleet maneuvers of that year. The vessel joined the First Fleet, First Carrier Division, on October 20, 1933; at the same time there was a change in command, with Captain Tsukahara Nishizō replacing Captain Kondō Eijirō. On November 25, 1934, the carrier joined the Second Fleet, Second Carrier Division, and one year later, on November 15, 1935, she was reduced to third reserve ship prior to being taken in hand for major modernization. The work, which has already been described (*see above*), was completed at Sasebo Naval Arsenal on August 31, 1938. She was reclassified once again as a first reserve ship on November 15, 1938, and one month later rejoined the First Fleet, First Carrier Division, at the same time as receiving a new commander, Captain Teraoka Kinpei.

On January 30, 1939, *Akagi* left Sasebo and took part in operations off South China until February 19, and after a further change in command on November 15, 1939, when Captain Kusaka Ryūnosuke took over the ship, the carrier left Ariake Bay on March 26, 1940, to participate in operations off central China until April 2. On September 5, 1940, *Akagi* steamed from Yokosuka to the South Pacific, where she supported army operations before returning to Kure on September 18, where she was registered as a special-purpose ship (*tokubetsu ekimukan*) on November 15, 1940. This classification remained in force while the hull and the weapons system were overhauled.

On March 25, 1941, she received her last commander prior to the outbreak of the Second World War, Captain Hasegawa Kiichi. She joined the newly formed First Air Fleet, First Carrier Division, as flagship on April 10, 1941. Leaving Saiki on November 18, 1941, she dropped anchor in Tankan (Hitokappu) Bay, the secret assembly point for Vice Admiral Nagumo Chūichi's attack group for Pearl Harbor, on the twenty-second.

In August–October 1927, *Akagi* participated in maneuvers at sea, during which operational experience for carriers' usage was gathered. Here she is shown in the center in Saiki Bay on August 4 with *Hōshō* to the left.

Carrier-based planes lined up on *Akagi*'s flight deck. This photo was taken around 1929, when *Akagi* was assigned to the 1st Carrier Division (Dai 1 Kōkū Sentai) along with *Hōshō*. Lined up on the flight deck are type 10 fighters and type 13 torpedo bombers (attack planes), with the former in the foreground. The structure protruding from the aft part of the flight deck is the aft aircraft elevator. This was a two-story structure with a lid on top called *Torii gata ōi* (Shinto shrine gate-type cover). The distance between the platforms corresponded to the distance between the hangars, of which *Akagi* had three. The elevator was complicated to operate because the ceiling height of each hangar was different, so the stopping position would have varied. The upper and lower hangars had a ceiling height of 5 m, and the middle hangar 6.4 m. With the lid level with the upper flight deck—the mooring position—the lower platform is said to have been level with the upper hangar deck. The lower platform (gangplank [*michi-ita*]) could not be lowered to the lower hangar deck, so in this hangar, partly disassembled auxiliary aircraft were stored. The elevator was electrically powered, but it seems that there were other ways of moving it. This type of elevator was later given up. Note the low position of the three 12 cm high-angle gun mounts on the starboard side, the wireless mast, part of the vertical funnel (*lower left*), and the maintenance personnel's waiting area (*to the right of the funnel*). The shadow in the background is *Kaga*.

Akagi at sea, probably in 1928. A very good photo of her, and the 20 cm twin turrets are now in place. She is conducting launch training, and on her flight deck can be seen type 13 torpedo bombers. The upper flight deck was 190.2 m long and 30.5 m wide, which was approximately 20 m longer than *Kaga*'s, a converted battleship. The triangular-shaped platforms on both sides at the forward end of the upper flight deck are antiaircraft lookout stations (*taikū mihari-sho*).

Akagi in a photo estimated to be from the beginning of 1929 to 1930. She is berthed at Kure Naval Arsenal, and this photo was taken by Rear Admiral Amari Yoshiyuki. After commissioning, the ship underwent maintenance and conversion works at her home port, Yokosuka, but from the end of 1928 to early 1929, she was again at Kure. This photo shows *Akagi* as completed, with a full-fledged closed upper hangar, two sets of windscreens at the forward end of the upper flight deck, and ten 20 cm guns.

A doctored photo of *Akagi* in 1930–31, outside Kōbe. The original photo was taken by Utsunomiya Shōten, and at the time *Akagi* was the flagship of the Red Fleet's Carrier Division (*Sekigun no Kōkū Sentai kikan*), which entered the port for the naval review (*kankanshiki*) in October 1930. On this doctored version, the ship is sailing, all masts have been deleted, and aircraft overhead have been added.

Akagi at Yokosuka in June–August 1931, in a photo taken by Hatakeyama Satarō. It is said to have been just prior to the Combined Fleet's departure and the formation of the 1st Carrier Division. *Akagi* was always moored to the buoy of the 3rd District. At this time, the southern end of Sankeien Garden in Honmoku, Yokohama, was rocky, and the naval historian (former lieutenant commander in the IJN) Fukui Shizuo has stated that *Akagi* was clearly visible from about 10,000 m. He continued by saying that when seen through a telescope, the rays of the sun and emblem of the warship's flag were beautiful.

Akagi during the special grand maneuvers naval review (*tokubetsu daienshū kankanshiki*) in 1933. On August 25, 1933, *Akagi* participated in the special large-scale maneuvers off the coast of Yokohama. In December 1931 she had undergone wireless-related renovations and other works, and in December 1932 she became a no. 1 reserve ship (*yobikan*). On April 25, 1933, she formed the 2nd Carrier Division (*Dai 2 Kōkū Sentai*) with the newly built aircraft carrier *Ryūjō* and participated in the major maneuvers. *Ryūjō* is here moored in front of *Akagi*'s bow, and on the flight decks of both ships, crew members are dressed in white second-class military gear (*dainishu gunsō*) to salute the passing *Hiei*.

Akagi on the day of the naval review off the coast of Yokohama in 1933. This photo was taken by the ship's flight department (*hikōka*). On August 25, 1933, *Akagi* was being prepared for the special naval review (*tokubetsu kankanshiki*), and it was rare for a naval review to take place during a period of intense heat, and the preparations were surely extremely difficult. Crew members are lined up on the forward part of the lower flight deck, and the guard force (*eiheitai*) is ceremonially lined up on the middle flight deck in front of the compass bridge. The staff of the 2nd Carrier Division and the commanding officer are waiting on the starboard side of the upper flight deck. It was reported that the visibility from the compass bridge was hampered by the 20 cm turrets.

Above: Part of the Combined Fleet in Tsingtao (Qingdao), China, at 11:00 on March 25, 1939, in a photo taken from Battery Park (the former German Iltis Battery). The 1st Fleet (*Dai 1 Kantai*) departed Kagoshima on March 22, the 2nd Fleet (*Dai 2 Kantai*) departed Sasebo, and the Combined Fleet (*Rengō Kantai*) arrived at Aoshima after breaking through a gale and conducted training. On March 25, the 1st Destroyer Squadron (*Dai 1 Suirai Sentai*) arrived at Tsingtao's outer harbor ahead of the main fleet and conducted battle training to secure the safety of the fleet's anchorage. This scene from Battery Park shows (*from the left*) *Akagi*, *Kirishima*, *Kongō*, *Kumano*, *Ryūjō*, *Mikuma*, and *Fusō*.

Right: *Akagi* in Sukumo Bay at 12:30 on April 27, 1939. The fleet had arrived two days earlier, and this photo was taken by Sublieutenant (technical) Fukui Shizuo from the light cruiser *Mikuma*'s starboard side.

A photo taken from the Italian light cruiser *Bartolomeo Colleoni* outside Tsingtao Harbor on March 28, 1939. *Akagi* is to the left, and the two light cruisers in the distance are *Kinu* (*left*) and *Abukuma* (*right*), flagship of the 8th Division (*Dai 8 Sentai*). The battleship *Fusō* is on the far right.

Kaga: Prewar Service

Kaga's keel was laid at the Kawasaki Navy Yard at Kōbe on July 19, 1920, as battleship no. 7 of the Eight-Eight Fleet Completion Program. The ship was launched on November 17, 1921, but the order to cease work on her construction came on February 5, 1922, and her hull was transferred to the navy on July 11, when she was taken to Yokosuka Naval Arsenal. Work on her conversion to an aircraft carrier officially began on December 13, 1923, in Yokosuka Naval Arsenal and was completed on March 31, 1928, at the end of the 1927 budget year, again according to official reports. *Kaga* was placed under the command of Captain Kawamura Giichirō at the navy station of Sasebo and was immediately classified as a fourth reserve ship (Captain Kawamura also received his commission on that date). In fact, work was by no means complete, and after being reclassified as a third reserve ship on June 15, 1928, and a second reserve ship on December 28, 1928, *Kaga* was transferred to Sasebo on the latter date, where work was resumed, the conditions of the budget being circumvented by including the work under "repair costs, costs of new equipment, and modernization." When the ship received her aircraft on November 1, 1929, she was classified as a first reserve ship and joined the Combined Fleet, First Carrier Division, on November 30.

The carrier left Sasebo on March 28, 1930, and saw service in the Tsingtao district until April 3. On December 1, 1930, *Kaga* was once again reclassified as a first reserve ship, and Captain Uno Sekizō assumed command. It was not until exactly one year later that the ship rejoined the Combined Fleet, First Carrier Division, this coinciding with the appointment of a new commander, Captain Ōnishi Jirō. On January 29, 1932, *Kaga* left Sasebo and steamed to Shanghai, on account of the first Shanghai incident, and beginning on January 31 protected the army's landing force. On February 5 her aircraft and the landing troops moved to the Shanghai Kōdai supply base. The fighting ceased on March 3, and on the twenty-second the carrier returned to Japan via the Terashima Straits. On November 28, 1932, Captain Hara Gorō took over command but was replaced by Captain Nomura Naokuni on February 14, 1933.

Reclassification as a second reserve ship on October 20, 1933, indicated the commencement of her reconstruction at Sasebo Naval Arsenal. Although the reconstruction officially lasted from June 25, 1934, to June 25, 1935, the work did in fact begin earlier.

After joining the Second Fleet, Second Carrier Division, *Kaga* again saw active service starting on November 15, 1935. After the Lukouchiao incident of July 7, 1939, at the famous Marco Polo Bridge in Peking, the situation in China deteriorated, and on August 10, 1937, *Kaga* left Japan, under the command of Captain Inagaki Ayao, to escort a convoy to North China via the Straits of Terashima. On August 15, 1937, the carrier arrived at Shanghai, her aircraft flying patrols over the city on the following day. An air attack on Hangzhou on August 17 ended with a disaster; the bombers lost contact with their fighter escort, due to the poor weather, and flew on to their target without protection. They were met by Chinese fighters, which shot down eleven of the twelve aircraft involved.

Kaga was ordered back to Japan to embark new type 96 Claude fighter aircraft and reached Sasebo on August 26; after taking the aircraft on board, she steamed out the following day. Until September 25 she provided air support for the fighting around Shanghai, and, among other things, her aircraft took part in the first aerial attack on Nanking on September 18, and in the attacks on shipping and army positions along the Yangtze. These operations provided valuable experience in the tactical employment of carrier aircraft.

On September 26, *Kaga* again steamed into the port of Sasebo for supplies, sailing again on October 4 for South China, via Makō, where she took part in operations until the twenty-fourth. She again returned to Sasebo on October 27, took on supplies, and left the harbor on November 1, escorting the landing forces that landed in Hangzhou Bay south of Shanghai on November 5. The carrier returned to Sasebo on November 17 and left again on twenty-first for South China, where she participated in the offensive around Canton from November 24 to 29, returning to Sasebo on December 2. At this point, Captain Abe Katsuo assumed command, and the carrier left the harbor once more on December 10 to take part in air attacks on various targets in South China between December 12, 1937, and January 21, 1938. Four days later the carrier was once more at Sasebo prior to moving to Yokosuka, which she left on February 28, 1938. She headed for South China, where, among other missions, her aircraft took part in the aerial attacks on Canton and Amoy. From October 12 onward she was employed in support of the occupation of Canton.

The return to Sasebo on December 12, 1938, was followed on December 15 by reclassification as a second reserve ship prior to a refit that included new arrester equipment and the modernization of and fitting new equipment in the bridge. On November 15, 1939, the carrier was reclassified as a "special-purpose ship," and the hull and weapons system were overhauled. Exactly one year later the ship returned to active service after joining the Second Fleet, First Carrier Division.

When the First Air Fleet was farmed on April 10, 1941, *Kaga*, together with *Akagi*, joined the First Carrier Division of this unit. From May 1 to 14, 1941, *Kaga* lay in dock in Sasebo; she then steamed to Ariake Bay on June 21. On June 31, she entered the port of Yokosuka, then moved to Tateyama, leaving on July 8 to return to Ariake Bay, where she arrived on July 11. On September 15, she received her last commander in Captain Okada Jisaku.

From November 11 to 14, 1941, the carrier was again in dock at Sasebo Naval Arsenal, prior to moving to Saiki Bay, where on November 17 she took on board one hundred torpedoes specially designed for the shallow water of Pearl Harbor. On the nineteenth she sailed for Tankan Bay, where she arrived on November 22.

Kaga as commissioned at Yokosuka on December 5, 1929. On November 30, 1929, *Kaga* replaced *Akagi* as flagship of the 1st Carrier Division (*Dai 1 Kōkū Sentai*), and the small *Hōshō* remained with the division. The 1st Destroyer Squadron (*Dai 1 Kuchikutai*) was attached to the division, and it was sometimes referred to as the "dragonfly-fishing destroyer squadron" since it had to rescue downed pilots. The background in this photo has been censored, but the stern of the battleship *Nagato* can be seen to the left. Despite being commissioned, *Kaga* still needed some additional revisions, so she remained in the arsenal's hands. In 1930 she participated in the grand naval maneuvers, and then she sailed to Sasebo Naval Arsenal for more fitting-out work.

Kaga shortly after commissioning in 1930. The exact location is unknown, but it is believed to have been a naval port. She was assigned to the 1st Carrier Division (*Dai 1 Kōkū Sentai*) of the 1st Fleet (*Dai 1 Kantai*) on November 30, 1929, and her aviation training was completed the following month. Note that the starboard 20 cm turret is trained almost 90° to starboard. The compass bridge can be seen just below the upper flight deck. *Kure Maritime Museum*

Kaga as flagship of the 1st Carrier Division at Yokosuka in July–August 1930. The commander of the division, Rear Admiral Edahara Yurikazu, boarded the ship at Sasebo on February 6, 1930, and his flag can be seen on the signal mast. In addition to *Kaga*, the 1st Carrier Division consisted of the aircraft carrier *Hōshō* and the 1st Destroyer Squadron (*Nokaze*, *Numakaze*, *Namikaze*, and *Kamikaze*). A Myōkō-class heavy cruiser, belonging to the 2nd Division (*Dai 2 Sentai*) of the 2nd Fleet (*Dai 2 Kantai*), can be seen to the right. The front of the forward funnel indicates that this is probably either *Myōkō* or *Nachi*. *Sekai no Kansen*

Portside view of *Kaga* at Yokosuka in July–August 1930. Fitting-out works did continue after *Kaga* was commissioned, and she did not join the fleet until November 30, 1929, and was assigned to the 1st Carrier Division, attached to the Combined Fleet. It was originally intended that she should have had three flight decks (upper, middle, and lower), but because the compass bridge, on the middle level, extended over the complete width of this deck, the use of this flight deck was abandoned. *Sekai no Kansen*

Kaga participated in the special grand maneuvers naval review (*tokubetsu daienshū kankanshiki*) on October 26, 1930, off Kōbe, after the special grand maneuvers (*tokubetsu daienshū*). This was *Kaga*'s second naval review, since she had attended the special naval review in 1928, during the fitting-out period. A total of 165 ships of 703,295 tons and seventy-two aircraft participated in the naval review, making it the second-largest naval review. This photo shows the crew manning the rail on the three flight decks. *Sekai no Kansen*

Overhead view of *Kaga* during the grand maneuvers in 1933. The maneuvers were conducted by the Blue and Red Forces, formed in May. Over a three-month period the forces exercised in the tropical South Sea and off Honshū. This photo was taken in late July as *Kaga* sailed through the Kossol Passage in northern Palau. This was the first time that all four IJN aircraft carriers participated in maneuvers (1st Carrier Division: *Hōshō* and *Kaga*; 2nd Carrier Division: *Akagi* and *Ryūjō*). Note the circle on the aft part of the upper flight deck, to mark the touchdown area of the planes, and the strips on the turret deck (middle flight deck), indicating angles. Carrier-based aircraft at this time were type 3 fighters, type 13 attack planes, and the new type 90 fighters and type 89 attack planes.

Kaga at sea in August 1932. The small bridge structure on the upper flight deck is said to have been installed around May–June 1933, and its small and unnatural shape in this photo suggests that it was added to the photo.

From late July to mid-August 1933, the 1st Carrier Division participated in grand maneuvers (*daienshū*) in the South Sea and off Honshū. This photo shows *Hōshō* (*left*) and *Kaga* (*right*) of the 1st Carrier Division of the Blue Force's Combined Fleet (1st Fleet), anchored in the Ulithi atoll. At far left is the oiler *Ondo* or *Erimo*, and the 2nd Destroyer Squadron is in the center (*Minekaze*, *Sawakaze*, *Okikaze*, and *Yakaze*).

A deckload of planes is spotted on *Kaga*'s flight deck during maneuvers south of Sukumo Bay on May 11, 1937. Three type 90 no. 3 fighters (*kanjō sentōki*) can be seen in the foreground, with type 94 dive-bombers (*kanjō bakugekiki*) and type 89 no. 2 attack planes (*kanjō kōgekiki*) behind. All planes are prepared for takeoff, and once the engines are started and the command for takeoff is given, all planes will be in the air within five minutes.

Kaga anchored in Sukumo Bay on May 11, 1937. During this time, *Akagi* was being rebuilt and *Kaga* was the major unit of the 2nd Carrier Division. Note that the 12.7 cm high-angle guns are mounted one level higher than earlier, and if elevated more than 30° they could fire on the opposite side, which was not possible earlier and never possible aboard *Akagi*. Note also the five 20 cm guns in casemates aft. *Maru Special*

Kaga in action in October 1937. In July 1937, the 2nd Carrier Division of the 2nd Fleet was ordered to Chinese waters because of the outbreak of the so-called Sino-Japanese incident. On August 10, *Kaga* departed Sasebo via Terashima Strait and, after having escorted an army convoy, advanced to the vicinity of Ma'an Islands, east of Shanghai, for air support. In addition to *Kaga* of the 2nd Carrier Division, *Hōshō* and *Ryūjō* of the 1st Carrier Division were also dispatched to Chinese waters. *Maru Special*

Aerial photo of *Kaga* in 1937–38. This photo shows the shape of *Kaga*'s hull after the addition of bulges when rebuilt. The maximum width of the ship was 32.5 m, but the flight was only 30.5 m wide, and this was one of *Kaga*'s special features. A type 96 fighter (*kansen*) can be seen on the flight deck. *Maru Special*

A rather dramatic view of *Kaga* in action in the South China Sea in 1937–38. A type 96 attack plane has just been launched. *Gakken*

A commemorative photo of warrant officers (*junshikan*) in front of *Kaga*'s bridge structure, taken between 1937 and 1938. The square windows on the front of the bridge structure are for the wheelhouse (*sōda shitsu*), second level; one level above is the compass bridge (*rashin kankyō*); and on the first level is the operations room (*sakusen shitsu*) and chart room (*kaizu shitsu*). The equipment in front is a searchlight controller (*tanshotō kanseiki*) and the sky lookout direction panel (*jōkūmihari hōkōban*). Also seen is part of the wooden flight deck and windshield. *Sekai no Kansen*

This photo shows the commander of the 1st Carrier Division, Rear Admiral Hosogaya Boshirō (*sitting in the center*), and his staff aboard *Kaga* on a photo taken in April–November 1938. Attached to the 1st Carrier Division was the 29th Destroyer Squadron (*Dai 29 Kuchikutai*), consisting of *Oite* and *Hayate*. *Sekai no Kansen*

Crew members aboard *Kaga* celebrating Navy Day on May 27, 1938. The person standing on a platform on the center elevator is probably Rear Admiral Hosogaya Boshirō, commander of the 1st Carrier Division. A twin 12.7 cm high-angle gun mount is visible in the upper left corner. *Sekai no Kansen*

Rice-cake (*mocha*) pounding in the hangar aboard *Kaga* in 1937–38. The photo is presumed to have been taken at the end of the year to celebrate the new year. The wings of several aircraft can be seen in the background. *Sekai no Kansen*

This appears to be a type 94 dive-bomber undergoing maintenance work in a hangar aboard *Kaga*, taken in 1937–38. The air-cooled, star-shaped engine has been removed. At this time, *Kaga* operated a mixture of type 94 and type 96 dive-bombers, but this is probably a type 94. The maintenance personnel are dressed in heatproof clothing (*bōwyo fuku*); some of them are stripped to the waist. It may have been a warm period, and the closed hangars must have been hot. *Sekai no Kansen*

A group of planes on *Kaga*'s flight deck in a photo from July 7, 1938. At this time, *Kaga* operated off the Chinese coast, supporting the army. Maintenance personnel appear to be moving planes from the hangar into launching position. The plane on the forward elevator is a type 96 dive-bomber, and forward of it are more type 96 dive-bombers and type 96 fighters. *Kaga*'s wooden flight deck is well shown, and the deck in the foreground is the same as before the reconstruction. The deck forward was added during the reconstruction. *Maru Special*

Kaga berthed at sea off the Chinese mainland between August 1937 and December 1938. This photo was published by the navy department (*Kaigunshō*) before the Pacific War, but the name of the ship was probably not disclosed. The forward part has four supports, but it is probable that the number was increased to six to strengthen the flight deck when preparing for catapult-related tests from the end of 1938 to the end of 1940. Note the rather dirty hull. The photo was probably taken from a Myōkō-class heavy cruiser.

The Hawaii Operations (Hawaii Sakusen)

The purpose of the Hawaii operation was to contain the US Pacific Fleet in their supply base at Pearl Harbor, Oahu, for about six to twelve months. The surprise attack, due to take place about thirty minutes after the declaration of war, was intended to prevent the US Navy from interfering with the conquest of Southeast Asia and the occupation and fortification of strategic key positions to form a strong defensive ring around the newly won territories.

The attack group sailed from the isolated Tankan Bay (Hitokappu Bay) under the command of Vice Admiral Nagumo Chūichi on November 26. The group consisted of six aircraft carriers (*Akagi, Kaga, Sōryū, Hiryū, Shōkaku, Zuikaku*) with a total of 441 aircraft (including fifty-four reserve aircraft), two battleships (*Hiei, Kirishima*), two heavy cruisers (*Tone, Chikuma*), the light cruiser *Abukuma*, nine destroyers (*Tanikaze, Urakaze, Hamakaze, Isokaze, Shiranui, Kasumi, Arare, Kagerō, Akigumo*), three submarines (*I 19, I 21, I 23*), and seven tankers and supply vessels (*Kyokutō Maru, Kokuyō Maru, Shinkoku Maru, Tōhō Maru, Ken'yō Maru, Nippon Maru, Tōei Maru*). The tanker *Akebone Maru*, which was also listed in Vice Admiral Nagumo's command group and is usually included by naval historians, did not in fact take part, since alterations to her connections for oil transference were not completed in time.

On the morning of December 8, the ships reached a point on the north route about 230 nm north of Oahu. Between 01:30 and 01:45 (Tokyo time), eighty-nine B5N2s (Kate), fifty-one D3A1s (Val), and forty-three A6M2s (Zeke, Zero), totaling 183 aircraft, took off from the carriers to attack the aircraft and airfields on Oahu and the ships in Pearl Harbor. This first wave reached the target at 03:25.

At 02:45 the second air attack unit began to take off from a point 200 nm from Oahu, and, fifteen minutes later, there were fifty-four Kates, eighty Vals, and thirty-six Zeros in the air. Two Vals, from *Sōryū* and *Hiryū*, and one Zero, from *Hiryū*, had to turn back because of engine trouble, leaving 167 aircraft in the second wave, which reached the target at 04:32. Details are given in the tables.

On December 24, 1941, *Akagi* returned undamaged to the western Inland Sea, which she left on January 8, 1942, for Truk, where the carrier dropped anchor on the fourteenth.

Kaga anchored at Hashirajima, the Combined Fleet's anchorage in the Inland Sea, on December 23, 1941; shortly afterward she moved to Kure and then sailed for Truk on January 9, 1942, where she arrived one day later than *Akagi*.

Pearl Harbor					
Number of Aircraft Carried					
Ship	Zero	Val	Kate	Total	Grand total
Akagi	18 (3)	w18 (3)	27 (3)	63 (9)	
Kaga	18 (3)	27 (3)	27 (3)	72 (9)	135 (18)

Number of Aircraft Participating in Attacks						
Ship	Attack wave	Zero	Val	Kate	Total	Grand total per attack
Akagi	1st	9	–	27	36	
Kaga	1st	9	–	26	35	71 (1st wave)
Akagi	2nd	9	18	–	27	
Kaga	2nd	9	26	–	35	62 (2nd wave)

Note:
Akagi launched a total of 63 planes and *Kaga* launched 70.

Organization of Air Attack Units

Attack wave	Leader	Aircraft	Carrier	Weapons	Target according to order of attack
1st	Cdr. Fuchida Mitsuo	15 Kates	*Akagi*	1 800 kg AP bomb Type 99 No.5	battleships
1st	LCdr. Hashiguchi Takashi	14 Kates	*Kaga*	1 800 kg AP bomb Type 99 No.5	battleships and carriers
1st	LCdr. Murata Shigeharu	12 Kates	*Akagi*	1 Type 91 torpedo	battleships and carriers
1st	Lt. Kitajima Ichirō	12 Kates	*Kaga*	1 Type 91 torpedo	battleships and carriers
1st	LCdr. Itaya Shigeru	9 Zeros	*Akagi*	2–20 mm, 2–7.7 mm MGs	Hickam Field, Ewa, Wheeler Field
1st	Lt. Shiga Yoshio	9 Zeros	*Kaga*	2–20 mm, 2–7.7 mm MGs	aircraft in the air and on the ground
2nd	Lt. Chihaya Takehiko	18 Vals	*Akagi*	1 250 kg GP bomb	Hickam Field, Ewa, Kaneohe
2nd	Lt. Makino Saburō	26 Vals	*Kaga*	1 250 kg GP bomb	Ford Island
2nd	Lt. Shindō Saburō	9 Zeros	*Akagi*	2–20 mm, 2–7.7 mm MGs	Hickam Field, Ewa, Wheeler Field, Kaneohe
2nd	Lt. Nikaidō Yasushi	9 Zeros	*Kaga*	2–20 mm, 2–7.7 mm MGs	aircraft in the air and on the ground

Notes:
Cdr. Fuchida Mitsuo was in overall command.
AP = armor piercing; GP = general purpose.

Aircraft Losses

Ship	Attack wave	Zero	Val	Kate (bomb)	Kate (torpedo)	Total	Grand total
Akagi	1st	1	–	–	–	1	
Kaga	1st	2	–	–	5	7	8
Akagi	2nd	–	4	–	–	4	
Kaga	2nd	2	6	–	–	8	12

Note:
Total aircraft losses were: *Akagi* (5), *Kaga* (15), *Sōryū* (5), *Hiryū* (3), *Shōkaku* (1).

Number of Aircraft Damaged in Attacks

Ship	Attack wave	Zero	Val	Kate (bomb)	Kate (torpedo)	Total	Grand total
Akagi	1st	3	–	3	4	10	
Kaga	1st	2	–	2	5	9	19
Akagi	2nd	1	12	–	–	13	
Kaga	2nd	3	16	–	–	19	32

Note:
At least 109 aircraft damaged from all carriers: *Sōryū* (22), *Hiryū* (?), *Shōkaku* & *Zuikaku* (37)

Ship	Attack wave	Ford Island	Hickam Field	Wheeler Field	Ewa	Kaneohe	Bellows Field	Shot down	Total
Akagi	1st	–	8	–	11	–	–	3	22
Kaga	1st	–	7	–	15	–	–	1	23
Akagi	2nd	1	2	–	–	–	–	1	4
Kaga	2nd	1	–	1	2	–	–	2	6

US Aircraft Losses in Attacks on Airfields Officially Credited to Akagi and Kaga

Results of the Attacks on Ships Credited to Akagi and Kaga

Target	Hits
Nevada (BB-36)	1 torpedo (*Kaga*), more than 6 250 kg bombs (*Kaga*)
Oklahoma (BB-37)	4 torpedoes (*Kaga*), 6 torpedoes (*Akagi*)
Arizona (BB-39)	2 800 kg AP bombs (*Kaga*)
California (BB-44)	2 torpedoes (*Kaga*)
West Virginia (BB-48)	4 torpedoes (*Kaga*), 3 torpedoes (*Akagi*)
Maryland (BB-46)*	2 250 kg bombs (*Kaga*), 5 250 kg bombs (*Akagi*)
Raleigh (CL-7)	1 250 kg bomb (*Akagi*)
Shaw (DD-373)	2 250 kg bombs (*Akagi*)

Note:
* Only one 250-kg bomb hit confirmed by US sources. It is probable that a near miss was judged as a hit.

A photo taken one day before Japan's entry into the war, as the fleet began to approach Hawaii. Photographed from the *Zuikaku* the photo shows (*from left to right*) the aircraft carrier *Kaga*, and the battleships *Hiei* and *Kirishima*. *Shashin-shū Shinju Wan Kōgeki*

View of *Akagi*'s flight deck taken in late November–early December 1941. This photo shows the port side of the flight deck forward of the bridge structure. As can be seen, the flight deck was wood covered and the black streaks are waterproof asphalt (*bōsuiyō no asufaruto*) filled between the boards. Three twin 25 mm machine gun mounts can be seen and, *in the foreground*, probably a 7.7 mm machine gun, likely taken from an airplane and installed temporarily for close air defense. The two ships barely visible in the background are the aircraft carriers *Zuikaku* and *Shōkaku* of the 5th Carrier Division. *Maru Special*

Akagi temporarily anchored in Hitokappu Bay in preparation for the Pearl Harbor operation. *Akagi* and *Kaga* (1st Carrier Division) departed Saiki Bay on November 18 and 19, 1941, respectively, and arrived at Hitokappu Bay on November 22. This photo was taken from a motorboat (*naikatei*), and the white spray seems to come from the waves. Several type 99 dive-bombers can be seen on *Akagi*'s flight deck. *Maru Special*

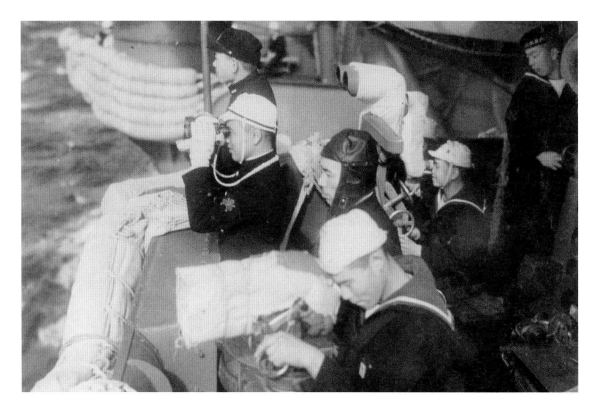

Watchkeeping aboard *Akagi* in late November–early December 1941. It appears as if this photo was taken on the starboard side, since a 4.5 m high-angle rangefinder can be seen in the upper left-hand corner. When advancing toward Pearl Harbor, the force was concerned about being detected by foreign merchant vessels as well as US naval vessels. Note the 12 cm high-angle binoculars. *Sekai no Kansen*

Akagi proceeding toward Hawaii. "Zero" fighters and type 97 attack planes can be seen on the flight deck. The "Zeros" are painted gray and have a single red band on the rear of the fuselage, and the "AI" on the tail says that the airplane is from *Akagi*. The type 97 attack planes are painted green, and they are armed with 800 kg bombs. The "white" lamps between the antennae are landing lights, which inform the pilot of the angle of approach. Note the folded wireless masts, the 12 cm high-angle guns, and the "pockets" (*poketto*) for the maintenance crew members.

On the bridge of *Akagi* in late November–early December 1941. This is a snapshot taken while the task force was on its way to Hawaii. The second person from the left is Vice Admiral Nagumo Chūichi. He was appointed commander in chief of the 1st Air Fleet (*Dai 1 Kōkū Kantai*) on April 10, 1941. He was originally a torpedo expert and had served as a commanding officer of various ships and squadrons, but this was his first aviation-related position. *Shashin-shū Shinju Wan Kōgeki*

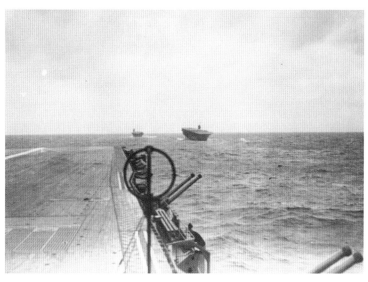

Zuikaku follows *Kaga* and *Akagi* at the end of November 1941 as the force was about to attack Pearl Harbor. Note the different island positions of *Kaga* (starboard) and *Akagi* (port). The Shōkaku class was designed with the position of the island bridge structure to port, but this was revised during the construction.

The task force sailing toward Hawaii on December 3–4, 1941. *Kaga* (*left*) is here shown with *Zuikaku*. The sea is rough, and *Kaga*'s bow is buried in the water. Aircraft are lined up on the flight deck, and the frame-like structure aft is the two-level aft elevator.

"Zero" fighters aboard *Akagi* during the Hawaii operation. In the background is the first fighter—AI-101—and in the foreground the fifth fighter. Each aircraft carrier had three fighters on standby for emergency launch. As can be seen, the red band on the fuselage does not go all the way around. Note the fuselage mooring cables. *Shashin-shū Shinju Wan Kōgeki*

A type 97 attack plane, with its flaps fully down, about to land on *Akagi* on December 7, 1941. This plane belonged to the first strike group. The landing hook is fully down, and the nose is raised in a three-point landing position. Of the ten arrester wires (type Kure, model 4) fitted on the flight deck, four (nos. 6–9) are in raised position. The three black lines in the foreground belong to a crash barrier (type Kūshō, model 3), which can be raised in an emergency if the hook fails to catch the wires. The control station was located on the port side at the aft end of the flight deck and can be seen in the upper right-hand corner. The man holding the flag is not a landing-signal officer (as in US aircraft carriers) but a *seibiin* (landing man), and his job is to guide the aircraft on deck when it has landed. Following *Akagi* is the plane-guard ship (probably the destroyer *Tanikaze*), which was to observe and rescue downed pilots—"dragonfly fishing" (*tonbo tsuri*).

"Zero" fighters of the 2nd Strike Group are prepared to be launched from *Akagi* on December 7, 1941. The lead aircraft have already started its engines, and the personnel are ready. Note the large battle flag on the signal mast.

"Zero" fighters of the 2nd Strike Group shortly before takeoff from *Akagi* on December 7, 1941. Engines are running and the mechanics / maintenance personnel (*seibiin*) are about to remove the wheel chocks. *Shashin-shū Shinju Wan Kōgeki*

A type 99 dive-bomber of the 2nd Strike Group takes off on December 7, 1941, while being enthusiastically cheered by *Kaga*'s crew. As can be seen, *Kaga* had her bridge structure on the starboard side, whereas *Akagi* had hers on the port side. The air crews preferred the starboard arrangement. *Shashin-shū Shinju Wan Kōgeki*

A maintenance crew member sits leisurely under the wing of a waiting "Zero" fighter, while *Akagi* is returning to Japan after the Pearl Harbor attack in early December 1941. It is a peaceful scene. *Akagi* lost five aircraft during the attack: four type 99 dive-bombers and one "Zero" fighter. *Shashin-shū Shinju Wan Kōgeki*

Triumphant celebration in *Akagi's* wardroom (*shikanshitsu*) after the Pearl Harbor attack. Among the officers lined up is Commander (Chūsa) Fuchida Mitsuo (*fourth from left*). This photo has sometimes been believed to have been taken when the fleet was anchored in Hitokappu Bay, but testimony from those involved says that it was during the return. *Shashin-shū Shinju Wan Kōgeki*

The celebration aboard *Akagi* seen from another angle. The wardroom was located on the port side of the middle deck. The first photo shows the view from the aft corner of the room, looking forward to the left corner, while this is the view from the forward right corner, looking aft to the left corner. There were eight tables in the room, and seventy-eight men could eat at the same time. *Shashin-shū Shinju Wan Kōgeki*

Commemorative photograph taken aboard *Akagi*'s flight deck upon the return of the task force to Hashirajima on December 24, 1941. Some of the individuals present were, *from the left*, (6) the chief of staff (*sanbō chō*) of the Combined Fleet (*Rengō Kantai*), Vice Admiral Ugaki Matome; (7) the commander in chief (*shirei chōkan*) of the 1st Air Fleet (*Dai 1 Kōkan*), Vice Admiral Nagumo Chūichi; (8) the chief of the Aviation Bureau (*Kōkū Honbu Chō*), Vice Admiral Katagiri Eikichi; (9) the chief of the naval general staff (*gunreibu sōchō*), Admiral Nagano Osami; and (10) the commander in chief of the Combined Fleet (*Shirei Chōkan*), Admiral Yamamoto Isoroku. *Shashin-shū Shinju Wan Kōgeki*

Rabaul and Kavieng

Vice Admiral Nagumo's ships were assembled at Truk to take part in the R operation (operations off the Bismarck Archipelago, in particular the capture of Rabaul and Kavieng) as a distant support group. Rabaul and Kavieng were key positions in the southern section of the defensive ring—against Australia and for blocking a push by General MacArthur's armies in the direction of the Philippines.

The group consisted of the same ships that had taken part in the Hawaii operation, with the exception of the Second Carrier Division (*Hiryū* and *Sōryū*) the patrol group (*I 19*, *I 21*, and *I 23*) and an altered supply group (*Kyokutō Maru*, *Shinkoku Maru*, *Nichirō Maru*, *No. 2 Kyōei Maru*, *Hōkō Maru*). The units left Truk at 07:30 on January 17, 1942, and reached the starting point for the first aerial attack at 05:00 on January 20. The start was postponed until 10:00 hours because of heavy rain, and at that time a total of 109 aircraft (forty-seven Kates, thirty-eight Vals, and twenty-four Zeros) took off from the four aircraft carriers. The aircraft found few targets; the seven defending Wirraway fighters (an eighth aircraft crashed on takeoff) were either shot down or had to make emergency landings, and only one aircraft escaped undamaged in the clouds. The Vals of *Shōkaku* had the greatest success in finding and sinking the Norwegian freighter *Herstein*. One Kate from *Kaga* was shot down by antiaircraft (AA) fire, and one Val from *Shōkaku* had to make an emergency landing on the return flight.

After the attack on Kavieng was called off at 10:30, Vice Admiral Nagumo reassembled his group, and the Fifth Carrier Division (*Shōkaku*, *Zuikaku*) separated from the main group. Their aircraft attacked Lae, Salamaua, Madang, and Bulolo on the following day.

On January 21, aircraft from *Akagi* and *Kaga* attacked Kavieng, which ended with similarly disappointing results to the attack on Rabaul; all aircraft returned. Rabaul was attacked again on the following day: the Vals bombarded Praed Point and put the coast battery out of action (two 15.5 cm guns), while *Akagi*'s Zeros attacked Vanakanau airfield and *Kaga*'s Zeros attacked Lakunai airfield. Two of *Kaga*'s Vals had to make emergency landings, but the crews were rescued. On January 23, three Vals and three Zeros from each of the four carriers flew aerial support missions over the landing areas but met no opposition, and all aircraft landed undamaged.

Kaga dropped anchor at Truk on January 25, *Akagi* on the twenty-seventh, and, two days later, *Shōkaku* and *Zuikaku*. *Shōkaku* returned to Japan the same day, while *Zuikaku* remained with Vice Admiral Nagumo's group. Details of the air attack units can be found in the tables.

Organization of the Air Attack Units for the Attack on Rabaul (January 20, 1942)			
Leader	Aircraft	Ship	Losses
Cdr. Fuchida Mitsuo	20 Kates	*Akagi*	–
Lt. Shirane Aya-o	9 Zeros	*Akagi*	–
LCdr. Hashiguchi Takashi	27 Kates	*Kaga*	1
Lt. Shiga Yoshio	9 Zeros	*Kaga*	–

Note:
Cdr Fuchida Mitsuo was in overall command.

Organization of Air Attack Units for the Attack on Kavieng			
Leader	Aircraft	Ship	Losses
Lt. Chihaya Takehiko	18 Vals	*Akagi*	–
Lt. Ibusuki Masanobu	9 Zeros	*Akagi*	–
Lt. Ogawa Shōichi	16 Vals	*Kaga*	–
Lt. Nikaidō Yasushi	9 Zeros	*Kaga*	–

Note:
Lt. Chihaya Takehiko was in overall command.

Organization of Air Attack Units for the Attack on Rabaul (January 22, 1942)			
Leader	Aircraft	Ship	Losses
LCdr. Murata Shigeharu	18 Vals	*Akagi*	–
Lt. Shirane Aya-o	6 Zeros	*Akagi*	–
Lt. Ogawa Shōichi	16 Vals	*Kaga*	2
Lt. Nikaidō Yasushi	6 Zeros	*Kaga*	–

Operations against the US Carriers

At Truk, Vice Admiral Nagumo's ships prepared to leave for Staring Bay (Celebes) to support operations in the Southwest Pacific. However, on February 1, American naval forces bombed and shelled several islands in the Marshall and Gilbert groups; these forces included the aircraft carriers *Enterprise* and *Yorktown*. This being the first definite intelligence on the whereabouts of the US carriers, Vice Admiral Nagumo decided to cancel the departure for the Celebes and attempt a surprise interception of the American group off the Marshall Islands, about 1,200 nm distant from Truk. Steaming eastward at speed, the Nagumo force consisted of the carriers *Akagi*, *Kaga*, and *Zuikaku*; the battleships *Hiei* and *Kirishima*; the heavy cruisers *Tone* and *Chikuma*; the light cruiser *Abukuma*; and the destroyers *Urakaze*, *Isokaze*, *Tanikaze*, *Hamakaze*, *Kasumi*, *Arare*, *Kagerō*, *Shiranui*, and *Akigumo*. His carriers had 180 aircraft aboard, which he believed would give him superiority over the US carriers, but at 23:20 on February 2, when his group was in position 8°N, 162°36'E, he received orders from the Combined Fleet to return. At 03:05 on the third, he turned 270° and retraced his course at 16 knots to the west, arriving at Palau on the eighth. On the following day, *Zuikaku* left the group and returned to Yokosuka to protect the motherland.

While engaged in changing her anchorage on February 9 *Kaga* struck an uncharted reef, and, although facilities at Palau were inadequate and allowed for only temporary repairs, she was patched up sufficiently to take part in the operation against Port Darwin.

The Air Raid on Port Darwin

After the conquest of Kendari on January 24, 1942, air attacks on the southern part of the Dutch East Indies became possible. The naval and air forces of the United States, Britain, and Holland had been pushed back to Java, a major target for the Japanese, and Port Darwin, in the North West of Australia, quickly assumed importance as the rear supply base and reception port for the retreating ABDA groups. From Darwin the invasion of Java could be disrupted by air and naval forces, and the Japanese determined to eliminate its port and airfield facilities by a surprise air attack, similar to that on Pearl Harbor. It was also hoped that it would serve to demoralize the Australians. The occupation of Port Darwin was also considered but had been turned down by imperial Japanese headquarters.

At 24:00 on February 7, Admiral Yamamoto ordered Nagumo to join the southern area fleet, and at 14:00 on February 15, the group—consisting of the carriers *Akagi*, *Kaga*, *Hiryū*, and *Sōryū*; the cruisers *Tone* and *Chikuma*; and the 1st Destroyer Squadron with light cruiser *Abukuma* and the destroyers *Tanikaze*, *Urakaze*, *Isokaze*, *Hamakaze*, *Kasumi*, *Shiranui*, and *Ariake*—sailed from Davao. They steamed westward from Halmahera through the Straits of Manipa into the Sunda Sea until, at 06:20 on the nineteenth, the carriers were about 240 nm north-northwest of Port Darwin. Here, a total of 188 aircraft were launched by the carriers (eighty-one Kates, seventy-one Vals, and thirty-six Zeros), which, after assembly, flew off in the direction of Port Darwin at 07:00, under the command of Commander Fuchida Mitsuo. The aircraft reformed at 07:45 over the island of Melville, with the fighter protection taking the lead, and at 08:10 Fuchida gave the order to attack. Between 08:20 and 09:20 the aircraft attacked ships, airfields, and other military installations in and around Darwin, taking the town and its defenses by surprise. The harbor was full of ships. Eight of them, including the American freighter *Meigs* (12,596 tons), the British tanker *British Motorist* (6,891 tons), and the US destroyer *Peary*, were sunk, and fourteen more were severely damaged; twenty-three aircraft, including ten American Kittyhawk fighters intended for the defense of Timor, were shot down or destroyed on the ground, while two more were damaged. The landing strips and hangars of the surrounding airfields were destroyed by land-based bombers from Kendari and Ambon, which attacked at the same time. Shelling from the sea set fire to the wooden houses, and the local people, fearing an invasion, left the town for several days. Port Darwin was thus eliminated as a supply base for Java, Timor, and Bali.

The Japanese aircraft returned to their carriers and landed between 10:40 and 11:40. The attack cost only one Kate from *Kaga* and one Zero from *Hiryū*, which was forced to make an emergency landing on Melville Island. The group retreated to the northwest, and at 13:06 *Sōryū* and *Hiryū* each launched nine Vals to attack a camouflaged cruiser that had been sighted near Cape Fourcroy (Bathurst) by aircraft returning to *Akagi*. The aircraft saw two ships at 14:56 at 290°, 32 nm off Cape Fourcroy. They attacked at 15:12 and sank the vessels, which were claimed to be a cruiser and a 1,000-ton merchant ship. In reality they were the American freighters *Don Isidro* and *Florence D*. The Vals landed on their carriers at 17:00, one of them being damaged. The group continued to the northwest and reached Staring Bay at 10:45 on February 21. Details of the air attack units are given in the table.

Organization of Air Attack Units for the Attack on Port Darwin				
Leader	Aircraft	Ship	Losses	Total
Cdr. Fuchida Mitsuo	18 Kates	*Akagi*	–	
Lt. Chihaya Takehiko	18 Vals	*Akagi*	–	
LCdr. Itaya Shigeru	9 Zeros	*Akagi*	–	45
Lt. Hashiguchi Takashi	27 Kates	*Kaga*	1	
Lt. Ogawa Shōichi	18 Vals	*Kaga*	–	
Lt. Nikaidō Yasushi	9 Zeros	*Kaga*	–	54

The 1st Air Fleet (*Dai 1 Kōkū Kantai*) assembled in Staring Bay (Celebes) on, probably, February 22, 1942. This is a view from the heavy cruiser *Haguro*, showing *Kaga* to the left and two Kongō-class battleships to the right. The fleet departed Staring Bay three days later for operations off Java. Note the supports below the forward part of the flight deck. It appears as if *Kaga* has six supports. It shows *Kaga* with six supports and platforms below the flight deck. This modification was carried out in 1940 with the intention to install catapults, embedded in the flight deck on both sides forward. In the end the project was cancelled and no catapults were installed. *Maru Special*

Just four days after returning to Staring Bay, following the attack on Darwin, at 08:30 on February 25, Vice Admiral Nagumo's group sailed once more. The group now comprised the air attack group with the carriers *Akagi*, *Kaga*, *Hiryū*, and *Sōryū*; the support group with the battleships *Hiei*, *Kirishima*, *Haruna*, and *Kongō*; and the cruisers *Tone* and *Chikuma*, as well as the 1st Destroyer Squadron as escort with the light cruiser *Abukuma*, the second group of the 4th Destroyer Division (*Maikaze*, *Hagikaze*), the 17th Destroyer Division (*Tanikaze*, *Urakaze*, *Isokaze*, *Hamakaze*), the first group of the 18th Destroyer Division (*Shiranui*, *Kasumi*), the second group of the 27th Destroyer Division (*Ariake*), and the destroyer *Akigumo*. From March 6 to 11 the first group of the 15th Destroyer Division (*Kuroshio*, *Oyashio*) was also under his command. Supply was the task of the first supply group (*Kyokutō Maru*, *Ken'yō Maru*, *Nippon Maru*, *Tōei Maru*, *Teiyō Maru*).

Vice Admiral Nagumo's task was twofold: he was to obstruct the supply of reinforcements for Java from Australia, Ceylon, and India and sink enemy ships attempting to escape. His operational orders alloted the task of attacking enemy fleet units and commercial shipping to his air attack group, while the support group was to assist and also attack enemy ships. The security group's task was to carry out reconnaissance and to protect and, where necessary, attack commercial ships.

At 08:30 on February 26, the ships had passed through Ombai Strait and were heading for their operational area south of the island of Java. The next day they received information that an enemy aircraft carrier had been discovered in the vicinity of Bali (US aircraft tender USS *Langley*). Vice Admiral Nagumo reacted immediately and hoped to be able to attack on the following day, February 28, but aircraft of the Takao Air Group damaged *Langley* so severely on February 27 that she was scuttled the same day. On February 28 a reconnaissance aircraft from a cruiser sighted an unarmed merchant ship and dropped a 60 kg bomb, which missed. The ship was not sighted again.

On March 1 the group was 140 nm distant, bearing 190°, from Christmas Island, when a Kate returning from reconnaissance sighted the US tanker *Pecos*. About ninety minutes later, the first Val from *Sōryū* attacked, followed by further machines that had taken off about an hour later. Nine Vals from *Akagi* also attacked, and the tanker was finally sunk after sustaining five hits and six near misses by 250 kg bombs. A total of eighteen Vals took part in the attack.

The Sinking of USS Edsall

A little later, the US destroyer *Edsall* was sighted by one of the three aircraft operating as aerial security for *Sōryū* and was reported as being a light cruiser. At 17:22 Vice Admiral Nagumo ordered Mikawa Gunichi to sink the vessel. *Kongō*, *Haruna*, *Tone*, and *Chikuma* turned toward the destroyer, and, eleven minutes after the order to attack, *Chikuma* opened fire at 21,000 m. At the same time, three aircraft took off from *Kongō* and *Haruna* in order to direct the fire. At 17:47 the battleships began to fire their 35.6 cm guns at 20,700 m. *Tone* joined the battle at 18:14 from 20,300 m. *Edsall* zigzagged violently, and although she often disappeared behind the columns of water thrown up by shells striking the water nearby, she received no direct hits.

At 18:00 eight Vals took off from *Akagi*, followed at 18:05 by nine Vals from *Sōryū*. Between 18:27 and 18:57 they bombed *Edsall* with eight 250 kg and nine 500 kg bombs, and, after suffering hits and near misses, the destroyer sank at 19:01. *Tone* did not stop firing until 18:42, while the battleships fired their last salvo at 18:59. In the battle, which lasted about an hour, they fired 297 35.6 cm shells and 132 15 cm shells. *Tone* and *Chikuma* used 844 20.3 cm and sixty-three 12.7 cm shells. If you add to this total the seventeen bombs, it is hardly likely that more ammunition could have been expended on a destroyer. Shortly after *Edsall* was sunk, the Dutch merchantman *Modjokerto* ran into the group and was sunk by *Chikuma* and destroyers.

Tjilatjap

On March 2 and 3 the group crossed into its operational area without further incident. At this time, Vice Admiral Nagumo's orders for the attack on Tjilatjap assumed it would commence on the following day, but bad weather, which was to affect the whole operation, necessitated a two-day postponement until March 5.

On March 4 a reconnaissance aircraft located a destroyer and a merchantman and bombed the former without success. Ten Vals, which had taken off immediately upon receipt of the sighting report, failed to find the ships due to the poor weather. Later, an aircraft from *Hiryū* found a burning freighter, the Dutch *Enggano*, in position 12°04'S, 108°l.5'E. *Chikuma* and *Urakaze* sank the ship with torpedoes at 12:43, after discovering that *Chikuma*'s armor-piercing (AP) shells passed through *Enggano*'s hull without detonating.

At 11:00 on March 5, 180 aircraft took off from the carriers, 230 nm southwest of Tjilatjap.[1] This was the same distance as from

Pearl Harbor, but in the opposite direction. The Kates flew at the lowest level, led by the aircraft from *Sōryū*, with the Vals behind and above them and the Zeros higher still. Eighteen Kates and nine Zeros from *Akagi* took part. As for *Kaga* and the other carriers, no information is available on numbers or pilots. It is known that none of *Akagi*'s aircraft were shot down, but again there is no information about the other aircraft. However, it can hardly be assumed that the thirty-two P-40s, which USS *Langley* had transported to Tjilatjap, had not yet been assembled, and in addition, Japanese reports indicate that AA fire was strong. In the air attack on March 5, which lasted about one hour, eight ships were sunk, and in the following days twelve more were scuttled; the town was taken by Japanese troops on March 8. Railway installations, harbor equipment, the auxiliary minesweeper *Ram* (at that time under construction), and about two hundred buildings in the town were destroyed.

At 10:30 on March 6, the group divided: *Hiryū*, *Sōryū*, *Haruna*, *Kongō*, and the 17th Destroyer Division (*Tanikaze*, *Urakaze*, *Isokaze*, and *Hamakaze*) steamed in the direction of Christmas Island, while the main group headed farther east but met no enemy. On the morning of March 7, *Kongō* and *Haruna* shelled buildings, oil tanks, radio installations, and a bridge on Christmas Island for about twenty minutes and then steamed off to the east. Aircraft from *Sōryū* located two armed merchant ships, which were sunk about 90 nm, bearing 300°, from Christmas Island. The two groups rejoined on March 10 and entered Staring Bay on the following day; Java surrendered on March 9. *Kaga* sailed on March 15, reached Sasebo on the twenty-second, and entered dock there on the twenty-seventh for attention to the damage she had received when she struck a reef on February 9.

Operations in the Indian Ocean

On March 24 the 5th Carrier Division (*Shōkaku*, *Zuikaku*), which had left Yokosuka on March 17, again joined Nagumo's group in Staring Bay, where preparations were underway for operations in the Indian Ocean. This followed a decision by imperial Japanese headquarters not to occupy Ceylon, which prompted the Combined Fleet to plan several raids in the Indian Ocean, including one against Ceylon itself. The purpose was to secure the newly conquered territories and to provide for supplying the troops fighting in Burma direct from the sea by defeating the British Eastern Fleet and destroying British airpower in the area.

On March 26 at 08:00, the battle group sailed from Staring Bay. Vice Admiral Nagumo had at his disposal five carriers (*Akagi*, *Hiryū*, *Sōryū*, *Shōkaku*, *Zuikaku*), four battleships (*Hiei*, *Kirishima*, *Kongō*, *Haruna*), two heavy cruisers (*Tone*, *Chikuma*), the light cruiser *Abukuma*, and eight destroyers (*Tanikaze*, *Urakaze*, *Isokaze*, *Hamakaze*, *Shiranui*, *Kasumi*, *Kagerō*, *Arare*), plus a train of six supply vessels (*Shinkoku Maru*, *Kyokutō Maru*, *Ken'yō Maru*, *Nippon Maru*, *Tōei Maru*, *Kokuyō Maru*) escorted by the destroyers *Hagikaze*, *Maikaze*, and *Akigumo*.

The ships steamed into the Indian Ocean via the Ombai Strait, took on supplies for the last time before the attack on April 3, and increased speed to 20 knots (from 9–14 knots) at 13:30, in order to attack Colombo on Easter Sunday (the fifth). The intention was to attack in the early hours of a Sunday, as at Pearl Harbor, but this proved impossible. On the one hand, British intelligence had fairly accurate information, and on the other, a Catalina sighted the group on April 4 and was able to send a sighting report before being shot down (*Akagi*, *Sōryū*, *Shōkaku*, and *Zuikaku* launched three Zeros each, and *Hiryū* launched six at 19:20; by 19:45, all aircraft had returned). However, the message reached Admiral Sir James Somerville at an awkward time and caused him to make a series of errors, with the result that, fortunately for the British, the opposing fleets did not meet. From April 6 onward the "A" and "B" groups had rejoined after embarking provisions at Addu Atoll.

Vice Admiral Nagumo should have left Staring Bay on March 21 and attacked Ceylon on April 1, but he was forced to postpone the action because of the delayed arrival of the 5th Carrier Division, which had been operating in defense of the motherland until March 16. Admiral Somerville had learned of this and had positioned his fleet to the south and northeast of the island from March 31 to April 2; after this he assumed that his intelligence officers had obtained the wrong data, and the fleet left the area to resupply.

The message from the Catalina gave Admiral Layton, in Colombo, time to arrange a heightened state of alert, and all ships that were able to leave port were sent to sea.

Akagi departing Staring Bay (Celebes) on March 26, 1942. Following the air raid on Port Darwin, the force sank the oiler USS *Pecos* on March 1 and then attacked Tjilatjap (Java) on March 5. On March 11, the force arrived at Staring Bay in preparation for Operation "C," the Indian Ocean raid. The ships following *Akagi* are *Sōryū*, *Hiryū*, *Hiei*, *Kirishima*, *Haruna*, *Kongō*, *Zuikaku*, and *Shōkaku*. It can be observed that *Kaga* was not present, since she had departed Staring Bay on March 15 for Sasebo, in order to repair damage sustained when she struck a reef at Palau. Note the sloping aft part of *Akagi*'s flight deck.

The carrier task force under Vice Admiral Nagumo is advancing in the Indian Ocean on March 30, 1942, as seen from the port high-angle gun of *Zuikaku*. *Akagi* is in the distance, followed by *Sōryū* and *Hiryū*, then the battleships *Hiei*, *Kirishima*, *Haruna*, and *Kongō* (*Shōkaku* is not shown). This task force was the most powerful mobile force (*kidō butai*) in naval history up to that time.

Akagi in the Indian Ocean in April 1942. This photo was taken from a type 99 dive-bomber just after launching. The white bow waves are dancing as the ship is sailing at high speed, and the large chrysanthemum emblem is conspicuous. *Kure Maritime Museum*

Colombo

At 06:00 on April 5 the airstrike took off. Of the total of 360 aircraft (315 operational aircraft, 45 reserve machines),[2] Vice Admiral Nagumo sent 128 into action. Under the command of Commander Fuchida Mitsuo, fifty-four Kates, thirty-eight Vals, and thirty-six Zeros flew to attack the ships, harbor installations, and airfields of Colombo. On the approach flight, six Swordfish of 788 Squadron were intercepted and fell easy prey to the Zeros.

Fuchida flew in a great arc around Colombo in order to approach the target from the north, and at 10:45 he gave the order to attack. The dive-bombers (Vals) began to bombard harbor installations and ships but were surprised by fourteen Hurricanes, which had taken off from an improvised runway on the racecourse. They shot down five Vals from *Zuikaku* and one from *Shōkaku* before being intercepted by the Zeros, which brought down six machines without loss.

Some of the Vals attacked Ratmalana airfield, from where twenty-two Hurricanes and six Fulmars had taken off. They were immediately engaged in aerial combat by Zeros, which succeeded in shooting down four Fulmars and seven Hurricanes for the loss of one Zero from *Sōryū*.

The Kates, hindered by the bad weather, dropped their bombs on barracks, a bridge, rail and harbor installations, and ships between 10:56 and 11:13. In total, the Japanese shot down fifteen Hurricanes, four Fulmars, six Swordfish, and two Catalinas and lost seven machines in return. They sank the old destroyer *Tenedos* and the armed merchant cruiser *Hector*, severely damaged the submarine depot ship *Lucia*, and slightly damaged the merchantman *Benledi*. Quays, workshops, repair facilities, railway installations, hangars, administrative buildings, etc. were also damaged or destroyed.

At 11:28 Fuchida radioed to Vice Admiral Nagumo that he should prepare the second air attack, and seven minutes later he gave the order to return: 121 machines landed on their carriers between 12:48 and 13:25.

At 13:00 a reconnaissance aircraft from *Tone* sighted two British cruisers, and at 14:27, after a second message from *Abukuma*'s reconnaissance machine, Vice Admiral Nagumo gave orders for a strike against these vessels by the ship attack unit. Seventeen Vals took off from *Akagi* at 14:49, eighteen more from *Hiryū* at 14:59, and eighteen from *Sōryū* at 15:03. Lieutenant Commander Egusa Takashige, of *Sōryū*, gave the order to attack at 16:29, and between 16:38 and 16:55 the dive-bombers of *Akagi* and *Sōryū* attacked the cruiser *Dorsetshire*, while those from *Hiryū* attacked the cruiser *Cornwall*. Both were sunk in textbook dive-bombing attacks, in which the hit rate reached the phenomenal average of 88 percent.

Trincomalee

At 09:00 on April 9, 100 nm east of Trincomalee, the air attack unit began to take off for the strike against that base. Vice Admiral Nagumo's group had been sighted by Catalinas on April 6 and 8, and, as at Colombo, the ships at Trincomalee were ordered to put to sea and to steam on a southerly course close to the coast. Among these ships were the aircraft carrier *Hermes*, the destroyer *Vampire*, the corvette *Hollyhock*, the tanker *British Sergeant*, and the auxiliary ship *Athelstone*. When the ninety-one Kates and thirty-eight Zeros reached their target under the leadership of Commander Fuchida Mitsuo, there were no ships in the harbor, and the British already had seventeen Hurricanes and six Fulmars in the air, having been forewarned by radar. For the loss of three Zeros (two from *Zuikaku*, one from *Shōkaku*), they shot down eight Hurricanes and one Fulmar.

Between 10:30 and 10:45 the bombers attacked the naval arsenal, barracks, oil tanks, AA positions, administrative buildings, and the airfield at China Bay, where they caused some severe damage. One Kate from *Hiryū* was lost, and there were two dead and one severely injured in the aircraft. The aircraft began to land back on the carriers at 12:30.

At 10:55, one of *Haruna*'s reconnaissance aircraft twice radioed the position of the British ships steaming southward, in particular that of *Hermes* (bearing 250°, 155 nm distant). At 11:00, Vice Admiral Nagumo gave the order to the ship attack unit to prepare for attack. Eighty-five Vals and six Zeros took off from *Shōkaku* at 11:43 under the leadership of Commander Takahashi Kakuichi. The carrier was sighted at 13:30, was bombed from 13:35 to 13:50, and sank at 13:55; ten minutes later the escorting destroyer *Vampire* was also sunk. The corvette *Hollyhock*, the tanker *British Sergeant*, and the auxiliary ship *Athelstone* suffered the same fate.

On the return flight the Vals were attacked by eight Fulmars between 15:15 and 15:40, which had been sent in from Ratmalana as fighter protection for *Hermes*. They shot down four of *Sōryū*'s Vals and one Zero, while the Japanese claimed to have shot down seven machines (Spitfires), although two of these were not confirmed: official British records state that two Fulmars were shot down.

Around 15:45 the aircraft began landing on the carriers, but, in the meantime, a group of nine Bristol Blenheim bombers had taken off to attack Vice Admiral Nagumo's group. Its position could be calculated with some certainty from the incomplete radio message received from the Catalina that had sighted the Japanese on the morning of April 9 and had subsequently been shot down by the Zeros of *Shōkaku* and *Zuikaku* at 10:10. The Blenheims did indeed find the group, surprised the fighter protection, and dropped their bombs onto *Akagi* and *Tone* at 13:25. Although they caused no damage, this was the first time that an enemy aircraft group had been able to penetrate the defense system and carry out an organized attack. The Zeros shot down five Blenheims and damaged another seriously, for the loss of one aircraft.

After the ship attack unit had landed, the group altered course to the east, took on supplies on April 10, steamed through the Malacca Straits on the morning of the thirteenth, and entered the South China Sea on the following day, where *Shōkaku* and *Zuikaku* separated from the main group to follow a north-northeast course toward Japan. As a result of the attack by Col. James Doolittle's B-25 bombers on April 18, the group was ordered to take part in the search for the American carrier battle group, which had been sighted by a picket boat. Vice Admiral Nagumo altered course from the northeast, but on April 20 the search was given up, and from 22:00 the ships steamed on a northwest course. At 10:30 on April 22, *Akagi* dropped anchor in Yokosuka Harbor.

Results of the Attacks by the Ship Attack Unit					
Aircraft (Vals)	Ship	No. of bombs dropped	Hits	%	Target
17	*Akagi*	16	15	94	*Dorsetshire* and *Cornwall*
18	*Sōryū*	18	14	78	*Dorsetshire* and *Cornwall*
18	*Hiryū*	18	17	94	*Dorsetshire* and *Cornwall*
2	*Akagi*	2	2	100	*Hermes*
11	*Hiryū*	11	9	82	*Hermes*
14	*Zuikaku*	14	13	93	*Hermes*
18	*Shōkaku*	18	13	72	*Hermes*
12	*Akagi*	12	12	100	*Vampire*
4	*Hiryū*	4	1	25	*Vampire*
6	*Sōryū*	6	1	17	patrol boat
3	*Akagi*	3	3	100	*British Sergeant*
3	*Sōryū*	6	5	83	*Athelstone*
3	*Hiryū*	3	3	100	large merchantman

Note:
Bombs employed were 250 kg Type 98 for ground attack and 250 kg Type 99 general purpose. It is possible that some near misses were judged as hits.

Organization of the Air Attack Units of Akagi (Trincomalee)		
Commander	Aircraft	Targets
Cdr. Fuchida Mitsuo	18 Kates	vicinity of naval arsenal
LCdr. Itaya Shigeru	6 Zeros	direct cover of *Akagi*'s Kates

Note:
Cdr. Fuchida Mitsuo was in overall command. No aircraft were lost.

Organization of the Ship Attack Unit on April 9, 1942		
Commander	**Aircraft**	**Ship**
Lt. Abe Zenji	17 Vals	*Akagi*
LCdr. Egusa Takashige	18 Vals	*Sōryū*
Lt. Kobayashi Michio	18 Vals	*Hiryū*
Lt. Sakamoto Akira	14 Vals	*Zuikaku*
LCdr. Takahashi Kakuichi	18 Vals	*Shōkaku*
WO Matsuyama Tsugio	3 Zeros	*Hiryū*
Flight Sergeant Sugiyama Takeo	3 Zeros	*Sōryū*

Note:
LCdr Takahashi Kakuichi was in overall command. Four Vals and one Zero from *Sōryū* were lost.

Organization of Air Attack Units of Akagi (Colombo)		
Commander	**Aircraft**	**Targets**
Cdr. Fuchida Mitsuo	18 Kates	buildings and ships
LCdr. Itaya Shigeru	9 Zeros	escort and attacks on enemy aircraft in the air and on the ground

Note:
Cdr. Fuchida Mitsuo was in overall command. No aircraft were lost.

Organization of Ship Attack Unit on April 5, 1942			
Commander	**Aircraft**	**Ship**	**Target**
Lt. Abe Zenji	17 Vals	*Akagi*	enemy ships
LCdr. Egusa Takashige	18 Vals	*Sōryū*	enemy ships
Lt. Kobayashi Michio	18 Vals	*Hiryū*	enemy ships

Note:
The Ship Attack Unit was not designated as part of the order of battle on March 19, 1942, but VAdm. Nagumo Chūichi altered his orders at 23:40 on April 4. LCdr. Egusa Takashige was in overall command. No aircraft were lost.

The lineup of crew members before departure was a kind of ritual. On the deck of the *Akagi*, flight crew members in their flight suits are lined up, receiving instructions. *Gakken*

Just before launch on the deck of the flagship of the Nagumo Fleet, the carrier *Akagi*. On April 5, the first air strike group for the Colombo raid was launched. *Gakken*

The Loss of Akagi and Kaga

Akagi and *Kaga* were sunk, together with the *Hiryū* and the *Sōryū*, at the Battle of Midway. There have been many analyses of this battle, so it will not be discussed again here. On June 5, 1942, *Akagi* was hit by two bombs at 07:24 and 07:25 dropped by Dauntless aircraft from USS *Enterprise* from an altitude of 500 m. One bomb struck the corner of the center lift, passed through the shaft, and detonated the torpedoes and bombs stored—against regulations—on the hangar deck. The second bomb hit aft on the port side and bent the edge of the flight deck upward. In spite of all the emergency measures taken (flooding of the torpedo and bomb storage rooms, use of CO_2 to combat the fire), the carrier became a sea of flames and after 10:50 was steaming around out of control. Around 13:00 the destroyers *Arashi* and *Nowaki* had taken on board the majority of the crew. After Captain Aoki Taijirō had given the order to abandon ship, the same destroyers rescued the remaining survivors, starting at 17:00. A radioed order from Captain Aoki to sink *Akagi* with torpedoes was canceled at 19:25 by Admiral Yamamoto, who ordered a delay, but at 01:30 on June 6, 1942, he ordered the ship to be sunk by the 4th Destroyer Division (*Hagikaze, Maikaze, Nowaki, Arashi*). At 01:50 the destroyers launched their torpedoes, and at 02:00 *Akagi* sank in position 30°30'N, 179°40'W. A total of 267 members of the crew were lost.

Between 07:27 and 07:30 on June 5, 1942, *Kaga* received four hits by bombs dropped by the dive-bombers of USS *Enterprise*. The first bomb struck aft on the starboard side. The second and third also hit on the starboard side, one close to the bridge and the other farther forward. The fourth exploded on the hangar deck, after it had penetrated the flight deck on the port side, slightly aft of the bridge. As with *Akagi*, the carrier turned into a mass of flames after bombs and torpedoes stored on the flight and hangar decks exploded, and petrol fires began among the fueling vehicles and aircraft. Here too, attempts were made to extinguish the fire with CO_2, but the fires were too violent. In addition, the fire extinguisher pumps went out of action.

At 14:00 the order to abandon ship was given, and the destroyers *Hagikaze* and *Maikaze* had taken survivors on board by 14:50. *Kaga* was finally scuttled by torpedoes fired from the destroyer *Hagikaze*, and *Kaga* went down at 16:26 in position 30°20.3'N, 79°17.2'W. *Kaga*'s casualties were probably 811.

Kaga was stricken from the list of IJN warships on August 10, 1942, and *Akagi* on September 25, 1942. With their loss began the beginning of the end of the once-proud Imperial Japanese Navy.

Commanding Officers, Akagi	
June 1, 1926	Kaizu Ryōtarō
December 1, 1927	Kobayashi Seizaburō
December 10, 1928	Yamamoto Isoroku
October 8, 1929	Kobayashi Seizaburō
November 1, 1929	Kitagawa Kiyoshi
October 26, 1930	Hara Gorō
December 1, 1930	Wada Hideho
August 28, 1931	Ōnishi Jirō
December 1, 1931	Shibayama Masaki
December 1, 1932	Kondō Eijirō
October 20, 1933	Tsukahara Nishizō
November 1, 1934	Horie Rokurō
November 15, 1935	Matsunaga Toshio
December 1, 1936	Terada Kōkichi
August 27, 1937	Moizumi Shinichi
December 1, 1937	Mizuno Junichi
November 15, 1938	Teraoka Kinpei
November 15, 1939	Kusaka Ryūnosuke
October 15, 1940	Itō Akira
March 25, 1941	Hasegawa Kiichi
April 25, 1942	Aoki Taijirō

Commanding Officers, Kaga	
March 1, 1928	Kawamura Giichirō
December 1, 1930	Uno Sekizō
December 1, 1931	Ōnishi Jirō
November 15, 1932	Okada Shunichi
November 28, 1932	Hara Gorō
February 14, 1933	Nomura Naokuni
October 20, 1933	Kondō Eijirō
November 15, 1934	Mitsunami Teizō
December 1, 1936	Inagaki Ayao
December 1, 1937	Abe Katsuo
April 25, 1938	Ōno Ichirō
December 15, 1938	Yoshitomi Setsuzō
November 15, 1939	Kubo Kyūji
October 15, 1940	Yamada Sadayoshi
September 15, 1941	Okada Jisaku

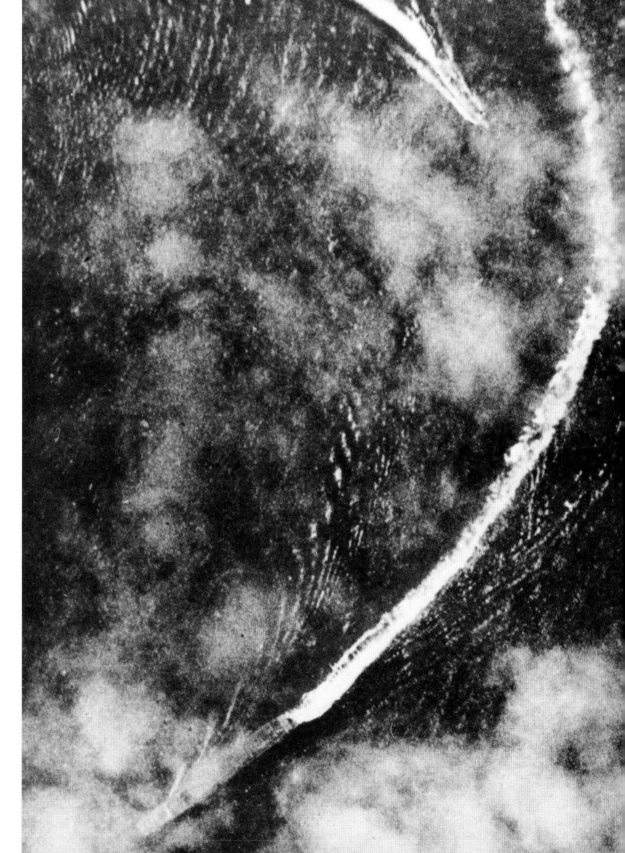

Akagi making a hard turn to starboard when under air attack by US B-17 bombers at Midway on June 4, 1942. The destroyer is probably *Nowaki*—the plane guard. No fighters are visible on *Akagi*'s flight deck, and the forward elevator is down. On the forward part of the flight deck is a large painted *hinomaru. Maru Special*

Endnotes

Chapter 1

1. It was three days before the Anglo-Japanese Alliance Treaty expired.

2. Mainly the "Four-Power Treaty," which concluded on December 13, 1921, and ended the Anglo-Japanese Alliance, and the "Nine-Power Treaty" (January 31, 1922), which restricted the defense of the Pacific Islands and had close relations to the "Five-Power Treaty," as the Washington Arms Limitation Treaty was also called.

3. It had been established due to the efforts of the League of Nations for disarmament, which proved unsuccessful.

4. Correct would have been this: "Stop the ongoing naval race to prevent the ruin of Japan's finances." The financing of the "dream fleet" (Eight-Eight Fleet), which the IJN had struggled for since 1907, was very slow, and the budget for the Eight-Six Fleet and Eight-Eight Fleet Completion Programs had passed the Diet only under the impression of the huge American naval expansion program of 1916. But the passing of a budget and its real financing were different processes, and in April 1921 Vice Finance Minister Nishihara Hajime was forced to tell navy minister Katō and sixty assembled high navy officials that the then-current state of Japan's financial situation was "fast becoming hopeless," and he appealed to them: "Whether it will collapse or not (live or die) is entirely up to you."

5. The chiefs of the delegations had agreed on capital ships and their ratios on December 15; the auxiliary vessels were treated thereafter.

6. The 5:5:3 ratios among the United States, Britain, and Japan were maintained, but in the case of France and Italy the original ratio of 1.75 was increased to 2.2. But this was insignificant for Japan because France had been deleted from the list of the potential enemies, and Italy had never been included.

7. Concluded in London in January 1902 and prolonged twice, in 1905 and 1911.

8. In his *Teikoku Kokubō Shiron* ("Historical deliberations on the defense of the empire"), Satō Tetsutarō, the "Japanese Mahan," had written by the beginning of the twentieth century that "particularly the fleet forces, capable to obtain sea supremacy, may never fall below the lower border compared with the strength of the potential enemies. This principle always has to be observed!" In connection with it, Satō pointed out the ideal condition of having the same sea power (strength) as the potential enemy countries. However, he conceded that this condition was unobtainable in view of the condition of the Japanese Empire. But Japan may not have been satisfied with this statement but had to struggle for a fleet "insufficient for attack but sufficient for defense." As a ratio between the attack fleet and the defence fleet Satō argued, "The attacking fleet needs more than 50 percent superiority against the defending fleet. From this relation, the absolute necessity is derived that the defending fleet has to have a 70 percent ratio at least against the power of the hypothetical enemy." Since that time, the 70 percent ratio vis-à-vis the fleet of the potential enemy was recognized as the minimum standard for the national defense.

9. As in the case of the genesis of the "standard aircraft carrier," the Washington Treaty also generated the 10,000-ton Washington "standard cruiser," which was recognized as "heavy cruiser" in the London Arms Limitation Treaty.

Chapter 2

1. The USN selected the battle cruisers USS *Lexington* and *Saratoga* for conversion into 33,000-ton aircraft carriers. The press at first reported that Japan would proceed likewise. Therefore, the American naval attaché in his report dated March 17, 1923 (serial no. 38, file no. 916-2500), doubted that the IJN wanted to obtain a displacement of 27,000 tons for their conversions.

2. The number that were "post-Jutland-type Dreadnoughts" had been four and five, respectively.

3. In January 1923, the Japanese press reported that the conversion plans for both ships were complete, and the work on *Amagi* had again been taken up since January 19. Even though details were treated as secret, the press reported the ship's displacement as 26,000 tons, the mounting of several 20 cm guns forward, sufficient speed to operate with the fleet, a takeoff deck forward and a landing deck aft, and a large capacity for the storage of aviation gasoline. These reports ended the puzzle about the intentions of the IJN, because the British magazine *The Navy* had still reported in September 1922 that as a result of the influence of the British Aviation Mission and the British views on the aircraft carrier, Japan had decided to build smaller aircraft carriers than the planned conversions of battle cruisers.

4. The damages were particularly great in the aft part, where also the keel had been broken.

5. The fitting of seventy-four faulty pumps in *Amagi* and fewer in *Akagi* and *Hōshō* and in the destroyers *Numakaze* and *Namikaze* had caused some agitation in the Lower House in March 1923. The opposition recognized a scandal and accused the IJN of being aware of these irregularities, incorrectness in the investigations (since October 1922), and general decay, and they compared it with the Siemens bribery case of 1914. However, a motion of censure against navy minister Baron Katō Tomosaburō could not be introduced, because the end of the session was declared at midnight of March 27 and the discussion had not yet ended.

6. During the fitting-out stage, on May 22, 1926, *Akagi* was visited by the then crown prince Hirohito, the later *shōwa tennō*. He was guided by Rear Admiral (constructor) Nagamura Kiyoshi, who also explained *Akagi*'s particulars. A summary of his explanations can be found in his reminiscences.

7. The Hamaguchi (Hamaguchi Osachi) government had decided to make financial savings and particularly wanted to reduce the military budget. The reduction of the naval budget automatically brought about retardations in building.

8. Measuring 152 mm in original plans but actually 127 mm. Source: *Sekai no Kansen* 944: 99.

9. Assumed to be the same as for *Akagi*, but the data are uncertain. Source: *Sekai no Kansen* 944: 100.

10. Of course, no main gun barbettes and main gun ammunition magazines were necessary, since it was an aircraft carrier, and such kinds of reconstruction work had to be executed inside.

Chapter 3

1. Workers and others participating in the construction called it "*Hinadan shiki*" with reference to "Girls festival" on March 3, at which dolls are arranged stepwise one above another.

2. Achieved in modern aircraft carriers by the angled flight deck.

3. Source: *Kaigun Zōsen Gijutsu Gaiyō* ("Outline of warship construction technique") 2: 232. See also Fukui Shizuo, *Japanese Naval Vessels Illustrated, 1869–1945*, vol. 3, photos 3058 and 3059.

4. Refer to the requirements for the conversion of *Hōshō*. The open hangar should be closed by canvas if necessary.

5. Note the removal of the island bridge of *Hōshō*.

6. Details will be given in the chapter on the avgas supply system.

7. The principle was similar to that used in the French aircraft carrier *Béarn*, in which the hot exhaust gases were mixed with cool air.

Chapter 4

1. Some Japanese authors have also stated that this ascent was chosen to adjust the takeoff-and-landing deck to the armor deck, but the authors consider this opinion to be unrealistic.

Chapter 6

1. Some Japanese sources also state 12 + (3) type 90 fighters, 36 + (6) type 89 torpedo bombers, and 24 + (6) type 94 dive-bombers, which equals 72 + (15), a total of eighty-seven planes. This seems to be more reliable at least for the first year after modernization.

2. It was the only elevator fitted with two platforms. The upper platform closed the elevator trunk so that planes could land, and the lower platform could be loaded in the upper hangar. In case of no flight operations, both platforms could be loaded, the lower in the middle hangar and the upper in the upper hangar. However, even though an advantage in theory, this method was very rarely applied.

3. In contrast to the combination of bridge structure and vertical funnel in aircraft carriers of the US Navy, the Royal Navy, and the French navy, the bridge and funnel remained separated, and the bridge was very small compared with foreign counterparts—

too small, in fact, and disadvantageous for operation guidance, as will be stated later.

4. The capsizing of the torpedo boat *Tomozuru* on March 12, 1934, and its effect on Japanese warship construction, is described in some length in *Warship 2011*, 148–66.

5. The report of the US naval attaché dated August 21, 1936, serial no. 957, states that in no. 3, "the difficulties at the conversion of *Kaga* [were] much larger than known publicly." Another aspect, which is often neglected, was the effect on the construction of other warships by the huge expenses the IJN had to spend for the (first) conversion and the modernization conversion of these two ships.

6. It is said that plans existed in 1933–34 to fit catapults for trial purposes. However, it is quite uncertain if such trials were conducted. Ground experiments with a catapult appear to have been conducted in August 1937. A photo of *Kaga* in Staring Bay in February 1942 shows the fitting of six instead of the original four flight deck supports at the bow. The addition of one more pair of supports indicates preparation for the fitting of catapults. The rumor that *Kaga* had catapults fitted seems to emanate from Mr. Osamu Tagaya, who mentioned that the pilot Kofukuda Mitsugi, in his book *Shikikan Kusenki* (Kōjinsha, 1978), said that for a brief period in 1940–41 a test catapult was installed on *Kaga*. In December 1940, when *Kaga* was at Sasebo, Kofukuda was designated to take off from the installed catapult, but when he arrived he was told that the test had been canceled because of a technical failure. The test was not resumed. While the strengthening of the flight deck above the anchor deck by an additional two supports can be proven by this photo, the fitting of a catapult and tests remain a "rumor," and the authors think that no catapult was fitted.

Chapter 8

1. The ships had, of course, different dimensions, and their armament and arrangement also differed. There were also other small differences, but these were hard to recognize for an attacking plane and are not mentioned.

Chapter 9

1. With the conversion of the battle cruiser *Akagi* and the battleship *Kaga* into aircraft carriers of officially 26,900 tons each, as permitted by the treaty stipulations, the required third aircraft carrier of 27,000 tons would bring the total tonnage to the upper limit. Consequently, only ships outside the treaty limitations could be built, and this was the background for the classification and tonnage of the "supply" aircraft carriers.

2. Chief of the naval general staff from December 1, 1920, to April 13, 1925; replaced by Admiral Suzuki Kantarō on April 14.

3. He took over this post from Admiral Takarabe Takeshi on January 7, 1924, who released him on June 11, 1924, and held this post until April 19, 1927, to be replaced by Admiral Okada Keisuke on the next day.

4. This session began only on January 18, 1927, due to the death of the emperor, and lasted until March 27.

Chapter 10

1. Remarkably, Japanese sources record virtually nothing of Nagumo's operations south of Java; even the official work by the War History Institute of the Japanese Defense Ministry *Ran-In, Bengaru-wan Hōmen Kaigun Shinkō Sakusen* ("Japanese navy offensives in Dutch Indies waters and the Bengali Gulf"), by Sasaki Masao, accords only six lines to this attack.

2. These are the figures stated in the above source, pp. 642–43. However, the total number derived from the war diaries of each aircraft carrier gives a total of only 275 planes (*Akagi*: nineteen Zeros, seventeen Vals, and eighteen Kates).